90 Lunch Box Recipes

- Healthy Lunchbox Recipes for Kids -

A Common Sense Guide & Gluten Free Paleo Lunch Box Cookbook for School & Work

© 2014 by Jane Burton

Published by Kangaroo Flat Books

- VISIT THE AUTHOR'S PAGE -

http://www.amazon.com/author/janeburton

ISBN-13: 978-0992543501

ISBN-10: 0992543509

ഇ൦ശ

Table of Contents

THE NUTRITIONAL LUNCHBOX

This book will give you loads of ideas for healthy lunch box recipes and have your kids eating and enjoying their lunches each and every day! It also gives a complete common sense guide to planning, preparing and packing nutritious lunches with many helpful tips and information. We lead busy lives, so getting the school lunch box organized is going to save time and give us happy kids. You'll love my stealth bomber super-food list too!

Appearance AND nutrition of lunch box food is important...here is why.

The Magic of a Healthy Lunch Box!

We know that food is vital to our mental and physical well-being. We also know that far too few children are enthusiastic about eating healthy foods when it comes to the school lunchbox. However, the trick is to send the kids to school with foods that are nutritious while still being interesting and tasty. This will help our children maintain their metabolism and their energy levels, hence being able to concentrate and have more fun during the day.

During the rapid growth periods from about the age of 5 to 12, we need to support this growth, especially with calcium, iron and protein. So, encouraging good eating habits early on can have a significant beneficial effect on kid's general health and overall ability to cope with the mental and physical challenges they will face throughout their teenage years.

Unfortunately, far too often the lunch box can be filled with high sugar, high fat and high salt foods because they are preferred by the kids and they are quick and easily bought at the supermarket. Of course, sometimes peer pressure comes into play, which makes it even more difficult to encourage your child to eat good foods. A lunchbox with a plain cheese sandwich and an apple just aren't going to do the job day after day, so let's look at some other alternatives. **Balance and nutrition is very important, but you need to be realistic.** Try to offer a variety of foods and change them up regularly. Fiber is very important too as eating many highly processed foods on a regular basis can wreak havoc with digestion and cause tummy problems. Learn more about nutrients in foods at the US Nutrients Database.

Food allergies and food intolerance can vary in symptoms and severity. An allergy is a response by the body's immune system. However, a food intolerance does not affect the immune system, but is believed to be caused by difficulty to completely digests foods. Of course this is why so many people look for gluten-free recipes. If your son or daughter constantly has a sore tummy and digestion problems then you should consult your doctor. Coeliac disease results from sensitivity to gluten which is a protein found in many cereals. Lactose intolerance is the inability to digests sugars in cow's milk. Many people turn to the Paleo diet which is based around eating natural foods. Paleo also focuses on eating nutrient rich foods. The general guidelines suggest removing processed foods and all foods associated with digestion irritation. This type of lifestyle diet, also known as the caveman diet, is a lot more gentle on the digestive system and general health. If you think this may help your child you can read more about the Paleo Diet on my author's page here at www.amazon.com/author/janeburton.

Good sources of iron include meat, canned tuna, chocolate, and dried fruits. Good sources of calcium include yoghurt, cheese, milk, tofu, canned sardines, flour and leafy greens. Making your own healthy drinks and freezing them is a favorite of mine, and the many options will be shown throughout the recipes.

This recipe book is in Metric and Imperial measurements however if you need help with measurement conversions, Google will help you convert measurements if you get stuck. Do a Google search "convert 1 oz into cups" and you will find a load of quantity options to select from the drop down box.

While the recipes are generally gluten free and/or dairy free, I understand that every recipe won't be right for each child because it depends on their particular allergy. **Pick the ones that make sense for your child.** Many recipes are Paleo, but not all for this reason.

FOOD PREPARATION AND OTHER TIPS

- **Allergies can be serious, so educate your child to not share their lunch and vice versa.** The main culprits predominately are nuts, eggs, dairy and seafood. Many schools now do not allow these foods in case of accidental allergic reactions. Contact the school, find out their policy and ask around about any other information that may be helpful to you and your child.

- **Use natural, low sugar fruit drinks or make your own juices.** I make a healthy, vitamin packed juice, freeze it in small bottles and put it in the lunch box. This serves three purposes; as a chiller pack, it helps save space and it's a healthy cold drink! (I even do this when I'm away from home and on the go) You can keep the weight of the lunch box down by including a drink doubling as a freezer pack. You can also freeze a half-filled bottle the night before and top it up in the morning. This way it will slowly thaw out during the day. If condensation and moisture is a problem, pop it in a plastic bag.

- **Chilling is important for any items that need to be kept cold such as meats, eggs, rice and dairy products.**

- **Choice of bags and containers are varied, but be practical.** Consider what fits into your child's lunch box. Only use container sizes you need, saving space and bulk. Consider how you will wash them or what may be better for the environment. Be sure they are suitable for the dishwasher if you do not intend washing them by hand.

- **Be sure the lunchbox, containers and bottles are easy to open AND close.** There is nothing more discouraging when the kids come home with uneaten foods because the lunchbox turned into a Pandora's Box!

- **Be sure the food is manageable for little fingers.**

- **Make foods easy to access and wrap up again.**

- **Encourage no waste.** Don't forget to tell the kids to bring home any leftovers for eating later... or for your pet or the backyard chickens to eat!

- **If making sandwiches, be sure they won't be soggy and fallen apart by lunch time.** This is definitely one way to get a lunch not eaten.

MY SECRET NUTRITION WEAPON

A Simple Idea with Excellent Results!

One of my secret super nutrition weapons is making my own **juice, freezing it in small bottles and sending it in the lunchbox as a cooler packed full of goodness and vitality.** So it doubles as a chiller pack AND a healthy, super V8 juice. Make blended juices that your child likes and "stealth bomb" in some high nutrient foods while still making the juice taste delicious. The healthy ingredients in homemade juices are known to get loads of nutrients into the body fast. So of course these are wonderful drinks to have in any lunchbox, or in the fridge throughout the day. The trick is to add about half fruit for sweetness and taste, then a handful of veggies with a dash of citrus for zing. Of course many other goodies can be incorporated too, which I suggest in my juicer book.

If you want some make ahead, high vitamin natural tasty drinks for the kids then check out my juicer recipes book. My kid's favorite juices include a balance of sweet and tangy fruits plus vegetables. They are surprisingly yummy!

LUNCH BOX RECIPE TIPS

Being creative could mean the difference in whether or not the lunch will be eaten. Think party foods for the younger children...it's all in the presentation! Bust out the cookie cutter if need be, let the kids help choose their shapes.

ADD A LITTLE SURPRISE!

Add a surprise to make the lunch box an enjoyable adventure worth opening. It may be notes or other little treats for the younger children. Think back...was there something you enjoyed seeing in your lunch box? Maybe add that!

MAKE PREPARATION FUN!

Get the kids to help if they are younger and want to get involved. This could be what it takes to make that lunch box come home empty! Allow extra time to pack the lunch so you aren't in a hurry and stressed out. Perhaps have an hour on a Sunday afternoon where you can prepare lunches for the following week and freeze them. **Show your approval if the kids help!**

These recipe ideas can be packed up and used for school lunches, or home snacks or lunches on the weekend. Just serve on a plate at home, or pack into your child's lunch box with cooling if required.

If your son or daughter has a favorite food, try to incorporate it into the recipes where it makes sense. If they have a food they can't stand or have an allergy to it, leave it out! Have you heard the saying "throwing out the baby with the bath water" In other words, sometimes adapting the recipe to suit your child's needs is better than no recipe at all! Same common sense approach goes with healthy lunches; don't overdo it because the kids may reject any healthy stuff all together :(

The recipe portions are laid out in standard meal quantities. This is good because you may want leftovers or need enough to serve a few children. They can go in the fridge for the next day anyway. Maybe you want to eat some for yourself for lunch! Another option is the recipes can be halved for lunch box recipes if desired. The freezer can be useful.

SUBSTITUTES TO THE RESCUE!

If you don't have a particular item you need in the pantry, use your imagination with swapping ingredients. You may need to do this if your child has allergy problems. If a recipe calls for cow's milk, use something else such as almond milk. Be aware however the taste will of course be different and not as "strong" as cow's milk. There is a lot to be said for good old natural traditional pastured full cream, not thickened or light...but again depending on the food intolerance.

If a recipe calls for sugar and you don't want to use sugar, then substitute it with your favorite sweetener like honey, stevia or dates. If you don't like using soy sauce, substitute it with coconut aminos. Same with flour, there are many options. You will be aware of your child's needs. You can buy gluten free from the supermarket easily today, if you use coconut flour it soaks up liquid in recipes compared to other flours, on the other hand, almond flour does not.

Almond flour is a favorite because it's high in protein. Apple cider vinegar is a mild tasting versatile vinegar. It and rice wine vinegar can be used in place of white vinegar. Red wine vinegar is popular in Asian foods. If you only have white, try using half the amount because it is more sour. If you want to make the carrot and apple muffins but don't have apples on hand, use a similar textured fruit like peach or banana. Tweak a recipe to make it your own, I do it regularly!

COOKING WITH ALMOND & COCONUT FLOUR

Almond flour is the number one flour substitute for many people that have allergic reactions to gluten or simply want to reduce carbohydrate intake (for example, followers of Atkins, Paleo or primal diets). From all non-grain flours, nut flours are the most similar to the traditional wheat flour. When substituting wheat flour for almond flour, usually the proportion 1:1 is good. However, you might need to use slightly more eggs (or vinegar, or baking soda) than noted in the wheat flour recipe, because almond flour does not contain starch or gluten and needs more binding ingredients for stability. When it comes to baking, grease the pan well or line it with baking paper because almond flour can stick just as well as regular flour. Also note that the textures of baked goods made with almond flour are usually more fragile, so let them cool to "set" and be a bit more careful when taking them out of the baking trays.

Coconut flour is higher in fiber, protein and fat than wheat flour. It is a very dense flour and very absorptive. This means a little goes a long way which is good news. Because of this usually a high proportion of liquid ingredients are required in recipes to counteract the absorbency. Don't rush in adding more flour, as you will see that after a minute or so, the mixture will "thicken". (If the end product turns out dry or crumbly, this can be due to lack of not enough liquid)

It is recommended to sift the flour before adding it to other ingredients because of coconut flour's dense nature; it can tend to have lumps.

There are often many eggs called for in coconut flour recipes. The eggs act as a binding agent and also often a slight raising agent. Although recipes vary, the standard proportions are about 6 eggs for every 1/2 cup of coconut flour as a rough guide.

DON'T STRESS IF IT DOESN'T WORK OUT

As busy mums and dads, the least helpful thing to do is to stress out because a recipe doesn't quite work out. Be reasonable, it's not the end of the world, if need be experiment because quality and products AND ovens are all slightly different. Go to plan B if you are in a hurry. Have a backup plan; make a quick and easy recipe instead, grab something out of the freezer or let your son or daughter buy lunch that day.

THE HEALTHY STEALTHY METHOD

Sometimes the "stealth method" if helpful, you can easily incorporate certain foods into everyday lunches while still having them taste delicious! Adapting certain recipes can help boost nutritional value for kid's (and adult's) lunch box meals. I'm often adding a handful of this, and a teaspoon of that in to the lunch box recipes and homemade juices to transform them into a "super food" meal.

Add ingredients where it makes sense. For example, I add chia seeds, flaxseed oil, greens, and/or dates to health bars, cakes or smoothies. Throw in some extra chopped vegetables to your savory recipes and fruits to your sweets. The addition of nuts, seeds, herbs and spices are wonderful too...get creative, many delicious recipes are born like this!

Throughout the recipes in the book you may find healthy stealthy ingredients suggested. These are of course optional as you know more about the limitations of what your son or daughter will or won't eat. **I found a gradual addition to certain foods using the stealth method is the key to nutritional success!**

Remember, if you take everything "nice" out, and put lots of "not so nice" ingredients in...don't be surprised if the lunch isn't eaten...would you want to eat it? Sometimes there has to be a compromise or balance.

LUNCHBOX PLANNING FOR BUSY MOMS & DADS

SUCCESSFUL PLANNING

The balancing act between your available time and creating a nutritious lunch box can be a challenge. However, a little forward planning can go a long way. Here are some tips:

- Write a shopping list: Before you go shopping, consider your lunchbox menu over the next few days. You will probably be able to plan much of your lunchbox food for the entire week.

- Consider leftovers: You may be able to incorporate leftovers from dinner the previous night. For example, you may have some chicken and couscous leftovers, you just need to get some wraps or fruit to go with these.

- Forward preparation: Try to prepare of as much as possible the night before. This ensures the stress of rushing in the morning will be minimal. Have the lunch boxes, utensils and plastic containers etc. all out ready to go. Some lunches can be packed the night before, which makes life a lot easier.

- Consider freezing foods: Freezing foods in small batches can cut down on time drastically. So be sure to consider freezing small amounts ready to be used when you need them. Just wrap them appropriately before you freeze them.

- Water is best for hydration in summer time: We now know it plays a vital role in concentration and just plain feeling energized. Headaches or lack of focus are commonly experienced when we do not drink enough. You can freeze half a bottle of water the night before school, and then fill it up the next morning. This acts as an ice block cooler to keep your food chilled. Healthy juices as an alternative will be discussed later. Giving both during summer time is a good idea.

PACKING THE LUNCHBOX

Packing a Successful Lunch

There are a few points to mention here. One is that **certain foods need to be adequately chilled** so your child does not get tummy troubles or a nasty bout of salmonella! Two is, **first impressions count**. If your son or daughter opens up their lunchbox to find it looks squashed or just plain and boring then they may not want to eat it. Of course children vary and you will know what your child is like in this respect. Try to keep the lunch box, visually appealing, easy to open and easy to eat. There is nothing worse than a lunch coming home because it was just too difficult to get to, or because it was squashed.

- **Include a surprise:** The lunch box ritual will be much more enjoyable if you include a little surprise, even just a few times a week. This may be a special little moist wipe to clean sticky hands after eating, a small special treat or a hand written note of encouragement. For that Christmas or birthday present you may want to include some nice cutlery or containers for the lunchbox...something unique just for them.

- **Keep it cold:** There are many choices available for lunch boxes and containers, including drink containers. Try to get a size that is appropriate for the needs of your child. You do not want a huge lunchbox in a small school bag; definitely one way to have a frustrated child. Unless the school provides a refrigerator, consider buying and insulated lunchbox. Of course another popular option is to use free frozen mini ice cooler packs, or use a half frozen drink bottle. I mostly use this option because this way there was no space wasted in the lunchbox, because the drink can be used throughout the day as it thaws out. On really hot days if you think the ice will be melted by lunchtime then you can freeze the entire bottle the night before. It is very important to keep especially meats and dairy food cold, so be sure chilling the lunch is done correctly.

- **Wrap it properly:** To make it easier for your son or daughter be sure to wrap the foods so they stay together and are easy to get at. If you think the food may squash, then use small containers instead of plastic or paper.

- **Wash the lunchbox after each use:** Be sure to wash everything thoroughly with hot soapy water when the lunchbox comes home each day. Wipe dry and have it ready for the following day.

- **The importance of drinks:** Today there are literally hundreds of options for bought drinks. If you can find natural drinks that don't have much added sugars and preservatives then these may be a great option. However, during the summer months, you should include at least one cold water bottle unless the kids have access to good water at school. And remember even if they do have access to it they may not use it. Drink fountains can be slightly unhygienic so packing that extra water bottle would be a great idea. If your child won't drink water, then it is better to have some form of liquid. Explore other options like natural, low sugar, low preservative cordials and juices. Make your own juices as suggested below.

- **Get the kids to help:** Of course not all children will want to help you pack their lunchbox, but some will and this involvement can make for a very successful lunchbox experience for everyone. Perhaps allow them to add one favorite thing to encourage their participation. Bribery…well, maybe just a little perhaps.

- **A balanced lunchbox:** Be sure your child's nutrition is being met in their lunchbox. Just think natural, interesting, nutritious and variety. Throughout the day and week you may like to divide portions of vegetables, salad, fruit, meat, dairy and starchy foods like bread. This may be a tall order, so if you miss something one day then add it the next. Similarly, if you give a unhealthy special treat one day, don't give it the next. Be reasonable and use common sense.

FOODS FOR BETTER HEALTH

FOODS LOADED WITH NUTRITION

It is an unfortunate fact that we are bombarded with artificial colors, flavors and preservatives in many of our foods today. **Try to minimize processed foods and incorporate as many natural, whole foods and raw foods into your diet as possible.**

This is a basic list of foods that are helpful to our health. (It's in my Juicer Recipes book.) I love this book because juices are a tasty, easy way to get high amounts of nutrients into the kid's bodies fast! **Firing up the juicer machine before or after school is not only refreshing, but a great healthy immune and energy booster.** Don't we hate it when the kids come home from school with a cold and then everyone in the house catches it! I have noticed a big difference in their ability to fight off the "bugs" when I use a variety of homemade juices regularly.

While many fruits and vegetables have a variety of helpful effects on our bodies, this is just a snapshot of a few, and some of the benefits they hold.

- Natural protein boosters for weight gain and vitality include egg yolk, nut butters, ground nuts and seeds, milks, soy powder, good quality protein powders and cottage cheese. Don't forget, using your muscles builds muscle!
- Almond flour is a favorite gluten free alternative to wheat flour as it is high in protein.
- Cabbage juice is good for the stomach and treating peptic ulcers.
- Leafy green vegetable juice can help it treating leg ulcers and sores.
- Beets are good for cleansing the liver, gall bladder and bowel.
- Natural sweeteners can be used such as soaked dates, raisins, and prunes. Date sugar, maple syrup, carob powder and raw honey are also good.
- Apple and pineapple juice are good to help cover up a "yucky" taste.
- Cayenne pepper is good for circulation.
- Alfalfa is good for bowel health.
- Anise (herb) will help reduce gas in the stomach.
- Citrus fruits, and any fruit/veg high in ascorbic acid help boost the immune system and fight cancer.
- Carrots contain beta carotene which help fight infection and cancer.
- Coriander (cilantro) is good for the heart and the digestive system.
- Dandelion is a mild diuretic.
- Dates are loaded full of fibre and are a great alternative sweetener to sugar. Great for constipation.
- Echinacea is a good detoxifying agent for cleaning the lymphatic system.
- Figs and prunes are a natural laxative
- Grapes are a good blood purifier.
- Kale is high in calcium and good for our teeth and bones.
- Lemons, oranges and grapefruit help eliminate catarrh, and boost immune system.
- Lentils are a muscle building food.
- Mangoes are good for the intestines.
- Milk is a complete protein.
- Lettuce can slow digestion, but is good for insomnia.
- Parsley is a tonic for the kidneys and blood vessels.

- Mint is good to help cover a "yucky" taste and also good for digestion.
- Pineapple is a good source of manganese and vitamin C, great for the blood and digestion.
- Pomegranate is good for urinary problems and is a detox blood cleanser.
- Papaya is good for intestinal disorders.
- Prunes are high in fibre and great for constipation. Also a natural sweetener in foods.
- Radish is good for catarrh.
- Sage is a good "wake up" herb and also good for the sinuses.
- Spinach is great raw in drinks, but don't overdo it because it contains oxalic acid.
- Thyme helps alleviate headaches, asthma and cold symptoms associated with the upper respiratory system.
- Watermelon is good for the kidneys and is a blood cooler.
- Watercress helps eliminate fluids from the body because it is high in potassium.
- Wheatgrass is high in Indole which helps prevent cancer. It is high in many beneficial enzymes.

Stealth Bomber Super Food List

What is a Super food?

Basically, **a superfood is a nutrient rich food which is beneficial for health and well-being.**

Here is a my favorite list of super-foods and healthy stuff I love to add into my recipes and the lunchbox wherever possible. The trick is to add them stealthily...no one knows, but the recipe still tastes yummy! With teenagers you can start to educate them that healthy stuff can taste good as well as be good for them. For example ask "did you enjoy those meatballs you had for lunch today?" if they say yes, tell them "that's great because I added some diced spinach". Let them know the extra things have been added when they have enjoyed something. Of course kids with food intolerance problems and allergies may need to opt for gluten free and natural foods only.

Although water isn't a food, it has to be mentioned because it is SO good for our health. I have a glass each morning to fire up the ol' kidneys! **Hydration in the form of water or other healthy drinks is essential for your son's or daughter's concentration and general well being throughout the day.**

Remember you need to be aware of any food allergies your child may have and work around it. If I'm unsure of a new ingredient or want to test something out I just add a little for the first few times. **Anyway, here is my nutrient dense short list of natural foods I add to recipes and juices regularly. Use them and your body will love you for it!**

- Chia Seeds
- Pumpkin Seeds
- Sunflower seeds
- Sesame Seeds
- Sardines
- Dark chocolate
- Berries
- Flaxseed Oil
- Goji Berries
- Cranberries (berries generally are great)
- Nuts (beware for those with allergies)
- Oats
- Dried Fruit
- Alfalfa Sprouts
- Leafy greens
- Apples
- Kale
- Spinach
- Mushrooms
- Dates
- Prunes
- Raw honey
- Fresh Farm Eggs
- Garlic
- Chili
- Olive Oil

Others: -

- Fresh home grown herbs
- Fresh home grown fruits and vegetables
- Fresh fish
- Fresh spices
- Banana
- Beetroot
- Cinnamon
- Mushrooms
- Quinoa

Food Allergies

Allergies commonly originate from foods like nuts (especially peanuts and Brazil nuts), eggs, berries, dairy, wheat products, oranges and shellfish.** The intolerance may vary. They may include; stomach pain and diarrhoea, nausea and vomiting, watery eyes and sneezing, swelling of the face, tongue and or mouth. If your child suffers from these symptoms or appears to be unwell after eating, especially on a regular basis, or from a certain food consult your doctor.

You may need to monitor, remove, replace and observe which food seems to be giving the problems. Always inform your school or anywhere else your child may come into contact with foods if concerned. With recipes, if in doubt, leave an ingredient out.

Educate your child NOT to share anything from their lunch box with others and vice versa. If allergies are a concern, tell them to ONLY eat what's in their lunch box. Although it goes against what we would normally teach our kids, explain to them it could make their friends very, very sick if they share their food. For younger children teacher help and supervision is required.

About the Recipes

I recognize we are all different with a different set of needs. **I have done my best to include allergy free recipe ideas, but there will be some recipes in this book not suitable for those with particular allergies**, so read carefully and don't use that recipe or leave out the offending ingredient/s all together if unsure! You can try using **alternative substitutes like Ener-G egg replacer for eggs.** Many of the recipes will include substitute ideas or simply say optional. **Dairy free milks such as almond and coconut milk are a good substitute,** you can check out my coconut milk and almond flour recipes if you need ideas. Different types of flours can also be substituted. **Nuts can be removed; use sunflower or pumpkin seeds for similar taste and texture, or perhaps add fruits instead.** I know if I'm unsure of something I only add a tiny amount to start with to test it out.

ALLERGY FREE SUBSTITUTES FOR RECIPES

Everyone's recipe and allergy needs are different, so please adapt, remove or substitute ingredients throughout the following recipes if required. I give options with most, but you will need to tailor some of the ingredients to suit your child's allergy, food intolerance or taste. Common sense prevails; if your child is allergic to nuts, substitute with seeds such as sunflower and pumpkin which also have that nutty flavor.

Common popular substitutes are egg replacer, almond milk, coconut milk, almond flour, coconut flour, or other gluten free substitute. Oat and rice milks may possibly be worth a try too. Coconut cream is dairy free. Check out what your local store has to offer.

These two books give you specific almond and coconut based recipes which are **dairy free & gluten free. Visit** http://www.amazon.com/author/janeburton

THE PROBLEM WITH SUGAR

Although many kids don't have problems with sugar "allergies" diabetes is a real concern if consuming too much. If weight is a concern use the more natural sweeteners such as Stevia and agave nectar in moderation. Remember however, these are artificial and won't break the vicious cycle of craving sweet sugary foods. The taste buds need to be "re trained".

To help with breaking the vicious sugar cycle, the Low Sugar Diet book by Peggy Annear offers answers and is included in the Suggested Good Reads section at the back of this book.

I like using dates, prunes and honey for healthy substitutes. Most processed store bought cakes, cookies and bars are loaded with sugars, so try cut down and make your own at home wherever possible.

LUNCH BOX RECIPES

If you would like an illustrated copy of this book, it is available in the Kindle version on Amazon. Each recipe is accompanied by a color photo of the finished meal or snack.

ROLLED OATS & HONEY SMOOTHIE

Banana is popular for breakfasts and in the lunch box because it is more like a food...filling, satisfying and healthy for kids. Smoothies are easy and quick to prepare when rushing in the mornings too!

Ingredients:

- 1/4 cup old-fashioned rolled oats
- 1/2 cup plain low-fat or standard yogurt or coconut cream
- 1 banana, roughly chopped
- 1/2 cup milk of your choice such as almond, coconut or regular
- 2 tsp honey
- 1/4 tsp ground cinnamon

Directions:

1. *Combine everything in the blender. Puree until smooth. You may add ½ cup of orange juice too if desired.*

COLD BUSTER CITRUS JUICE

Juices are beneficial to get nutrients and vitamins into the body fast! They are a great energy booster and work really well in the lunch box because they can be frozen beforehand if desired, then double as a chiller pack and a refreshing drink.

Don't we hate it when the kids come home with a cold they caught from their best friends! Help prevent and treat a cold with this powerful vitamin cocktail.

Ingredients:

- 2 oranges, peeled and quartered
- 1/2 grapefruit, peeled (if too sour for your child, use 2 kiwi fruits instead)
- 1/2 lemon, peeled but keep about a tsp size of peel (optional)
- 1/2 lime, peeled

Directions:

1. *Peel fruits, but keep 1/4 of the lemon peel on if the kids taste buds can handle it for extra cold fighting properties. Push through the juicer and freeze as a chiller bottle ready for the lunch box.*

My kids love it like this. Lemon peels are full of super-flavonoids. I find this recipe can be hard on the tummy, so eat something with it, or dilute with water. Refreshing summer time drink and a soother for winter colds!

PINEAPPLE AND ORANGE SMOOTHIE

Ginger aids digestion, orange is a good starter. Great morning or lunch smoothie that's extra refreshing! Put half of it in a bottle for the chilled lunchbox.

Ingredients:

- 12 oz fresh orange juice
- 1/2 cup drained pineapple chunks or pieces
- 1 ¼ cups vanilla yoghurt
- 1/4 tsp finely grated ginger if your child likes it (optional)

Directions:

1. *Combine all ingredients in blender and blend on high till smooth and frothy.*

Ginger is great for digestion and nausea. Garnish with a slice of favorite fruit or partially freeze and use a chilled drink.

SALAMI & CHICK PEA SUPER SALAD

This is a non Paleo Recipe, but none the less an excellent source of nutrition for lunches on occasion.

Ingredients:

- 1 small can of chickpeas, rinsed and thoroughly drained
- 1/2 - 1 cup grape or cherry tomatoes, halved
- about 1 roasted capsicum, thinly sliced
- about 2 cups of baby spinach & rocket leafy mix
- about 1 cup shaved spicy natural salami, cut into thick strips (optional)
- 2 tsp pepitas (pumpkin seeds)
- Separate - 2 tsp balsamic vinegar for dressing

*Switch it to Paleo by adding crispy fried bacon pieces, leave out the chick peas, and add a handful of sunflower seeds.

Directions:

1. *Combine the chickpeas, tomato, capsicum, spinach and rocket, salami and pepitas in a bowl.*
2. *Pack the salad into chilled lunch box and have the dressing in a separate container. Pour over when ready to eat.*

LENTIL & AVOCADO SALAD

Ingredients:

- 1 - 2 avocados, chopped
- 1 small onion or shallots, chopped
- about 1 small cup of rinsed and cooked lentils (bought are okay)
- 1 cup of cherry tomatoes, chopped
- Mixed fresh herbs
- 1 cup leafy greens of your choice. I like baby spinach and lettuce combo
- 1/2 cup crumbled fetta cheese (optional)
- Ground black pepper to taste

* Add nuts too if your child likes them.

Directions:

1. *Prepare all ingredients and toss together. Place in container ready for the lunch box. Colorful and intriguing!*

GREEN MONSTER SMOOTHIE CUPS

Ingredients:

- 1 cup fresh kale or baby spinach, washed (spinach works too)
- 1 mangoes or 2 apples (for sweetness)
- 1 banana, peeled and chopped
- juice from 1/2 a lemon or lime
- 1 kiwifruit, peeled and chopped

*Use the stealth bombing method to add 1 tsp chia seeds and 1 tsp flaxseed oil. Have for breakfast, lunch OR half frozen in the lunch box!

Directions:

1. *Process all ingredients in a blender until well mixed. Pour into sealed cups/containers and refrigerate before packing into the lunch box.*

If you partially freeze, this can be used as a chiller pack for the lunch. Simple, healthy and delicious!

CHICKEN AND GREEN GRAPE SALAD

Ingredients:

- 4 chicken breasts, boneless and skinless, cut in bite size pieces
- 2 cups green grapes
- ½ cup celery stalks, sliced
- ¼ cup natural mayonnaise
- 2 Tbsp honey
- 1 Tbsp curry powder
- salt and black pepper to taste

Directions:

1. *Preheat the oven to 350° F (180° C)*
2. *Cover your baking sheet with aluminum foil. Place the chicken pieces on it and cook for 10 minutes.*
3. *Flip the chicken pieces over and cook for 10 more minutes. Then let them cool down a bit.*
4. *In a bowl mix the chicken pieces together with grapes and celery.*
5. *In a smaller bowl combine mayonnaise with honey and curry. Mix the sauce in the salad.*

*Keep all meats and dairy well chilled.

HAM ROLY POLYS

Ingredients:

- 12 slices ham
- 1 big cucumber, sliced
- 1 cup lettuce leaves, chopped.
- ¼ cup Paleo mayonnaise
- 3 Tbsp mustard
- 3 Tbsp raw honey
- salt and pepper to taste

Directions:

1. *In a small bowl combine mayonnaise with mustard, raw honey, salt and pepper.*
2. *Spread each ham slice from one side with the sauce.*
3. *Mix the cucumber slices with lettuce. Stuff each roll with this mix.*
4. *Serve as lunch at home or pop them in the lunch box with a cooler.*

PLUM JUICE TUMMY TONIC

This recipe came from my Juice book. It is great for alleviating constipation. There are many juices inside that help alleviate common ailments that kids often suffer on occasion, so take a look.

Ingredients:

- 3 pitted plums (prunes are good too, but blend first in 1/2 cup of water)
- 2 apples, chopped
- 1 pear, halved

Directions:

1. *Juice all together if using plums. If using prunes, juice the apple and pear alternately, then add to the blended prune juice.*

2. *Drink in the morning, or freeze and make into a chiller bottle for lunches.*

Apple and pears have good fibre and prunes have a laxative effect. A great tonic for digestion!

LUNCHBOX CHICKEN NUGGETS

*If preferred, you can use more chicken and that way you will have less crumb mixture.

Ingredients:

- 3 chicken breasts, boneless and skinless
- 7oz (200g) gluten free crackers, ground to crumbs
- 1 cup nutritional yeast
- 1/4 cup almond flour
- 1/4 cup arrowroot powder
- dried mustard powder to taste (optional)
- 3 eggs
- 3 Tbsp olive oil
- salt and pepper to taste

Directions:

1. *Preheat the oven to 400° F or 200° C*
2. *Place the chicken breasts between two sheets of parchment paper and pound it down to about ½inch (1cm) thickness. Cut the meat into 2x2 inch nuggets (5x5 cm).*
3. *Have 3 shallow bowls next to your prepared baking sheets. One bowl contains mixed almond flour, arrowroot starch, salt and pepper. In the second bowl is a mix of mustard, eggs and olive oil. The third bowl has a mix of gluten free cracker crumbs combined with nutritional yeast.*
4. *Take each piece of chicken and dip them in the bowls in the order described in the previous step. Put each of coated nugget on the baking sheets.*
5. *Cook for 20 minutes. For real crispiness, set the oven on high heat and cook for 2 more minutes.*

APPLE CHIPS

Ingredients:

- 2 large apples
- 2 cups apple juice
- 1 cinnamon stick

Directions:

1. *Preheat oven to 250 F (120 C)*
2. *In a pot combine apple juice and cinnamon stick. Bring it to boil.*
3. *Remove the apple cores and slice the apples crosswise to create chips.*
4. *Carefully put the apple slices in the boiling juice and cook for 5 minutes.*
5. *Take the apple slices out of the juice and place on a cloth. Pat dry.*
6. *Place the apple slices on a wire cooling rack placed on a baking sheet.*
7. *Bake the apple slices for 35-40 minutes until they dry completely.*
8. *Let them cool before putting into a container.*

PEANUT BUTTER BANANA SMOOTHIE

A yummy banana, nutritious nutty smoothie treat. For kids with a nut allergy, leave out the nuts and use chocolate instead.

Ingredients:

- 2 bananas, peeled and roughly chopped
- 1/4 cup peanut butter and/or chocolate pieces
- 1 cup of milk you prefer such as whole, skim, almond or coconut etc.
- 1 tsp honey or maple syrup
- 2 tsp ground hazelnuts or almonds (optional)

*You can stealth bomb in some chia or sunflower seeds for extra goodness.

Directions:

1. *Combine everything in a blender. Blend until smooth. Serve for a satisfying low GI breakfast before school, or freeze ready for the lunch box. This one will get them through till lunch time!*

BOLOGNA SAUSAGE WRAPS

Clearly these are for the fussy, plain eater. Try to incorporate variety into the wrap gradually, or add something else like cheese, veg, dip or fruit as a side.

Ingredients:

Bologna sausage, Devon or other meat from the supermarket, sliced (natural or cold meats for Paleo)
Gluten free wraps of your choice
Cheese slices of choice (If your child can't eat, or doesn't want cheese add variety with the accompaniment)
* You may like to add your child's favorite meat, spread or salad to these.

Directions:

None really, just layer and wrap it up into rolls. Hold in place with toothpicks or paper or cling wrap if needed. Cut into manageable sized pieces for the lunch box. This is a base; it's flexible with what you add. It goes well with dips and salads.

AVOCADO AND EGG SALAD

* If eggs aren't allowed at your school due to allergies, save this recipe for lunch at home.

Ingredients:

- 4 hard boiled eggs (I add more if the backyard chickens have paid plenty!)
- 1 avocado
- ¼ cup spinach leaves, roughly chopped
- ¼ cup walnuts, roughly chopped (pumpkin seeds work too)
- 1 Tbsp lemon juice
- 1 Tbsp mustard
- salt and black pepper to taste

Directions:

1. *Mix the spinach and walnuts together.*
2. *Cut the eggs and avocado in pieces. Put them on top of the salad.*
3. *In a separate bowl mix the lemon juice, mustard, salt and pepper. Sprinkle the juice over salad. Enjoy!*

ASIAN CHICKEN LETTUCE WRAP

Ingredients:

- 1 lb (450g) boneless, skinless chicken breasts, finely chopped
- 1/2 lb (250g) button mushrooms, chopped
- 8 iceberg lettuce leaves
- 1/2 cup chestnuts, minced
- 1/4 cup roasted cashew nuts, coarsely chopped
- 1 onion, minced
- 2 cloves garlic, minced
- 3 Tbsp olive oil
- 2 Tbsp soy sauce
- 2 Tbsp red wine vinegar
- 1 Tbsp Hoisin sauce
- 2 tsp fresh ginger, minced

- salt and black pepper to taste

Directions:

1. *Mix the soy sauce, Hoisin sauce, apple cider vinegar and salt in a small bowl.*
2. *Heat the oil. Add the chicken and stir fry until almost done. This could take about 5 minutes.*
3. *Then add the garlic, onion, mushrooms, chestnuts and ginger. Fry for 2 more minutes and stir until the mixture is done.*
4. *Scoop the filling into lettuce cups. Can pack lettuce leaves in a separate container in the lunch box and let the kids load it up with the filling.*

CHICKEN EGG FAMILY

Cutest little chickens ever! Perfect for kid's Paleo lunch idea! Great for fussy eaters! If eggs aren't allowed at your school, save this recipe for home.

Ingredients:

- Hard boiled eggs
- Carrots
- Peppercorns, raisins or sultanas
- Salad greens, spinach leaves or herbs

Directions:

1. Cut carrots into shapes – chicken combs & beaks for adult chickens.
2. Adult Chickens: Trim the base of hard boiled egg so it will stand upright. Make a small slit at top of egg for chicken comb and one in center for the beak as well as two smaller ones for eyes. Push carrot comb and beak into place and peppercorns for the eyes.
3. Chicks: Carefully cut a zigzag pattern around middle of egg without penetrating the yolk at all. Remove the top section zigzagged egg white 'shell' and cut small holes into yolk for chick's beak and eyes. Push carrot and peppercorns or raisins into place. (Unused boiled egg whites may be used in salads, etc)
4. Serve on nests of salad greens / spinach leaves and add some grated

carrots, salad onion and herbs. All the little chickadees say cheep, cheep! Of course adding a few slices of cold meat on the side is even better for a lunch box meal!

Yummy Pork Patties

Ingredients:

- 1lb (450 g) lean pork, ground
- 1 tsp sage
- 1 tsp salt
- 1 tsp paprika powder
- ½ tsp fresh black pepper, ground

*Stealth bomb in some finely diced kale or spinach.

Directions:

1. *In a small bowl mix all spices.*
2. *Add this mixture to the ground pork. Blend well.*
3. *Fry the patties in a skillet on medium heat until they are golden brown.*

Easy Quinoa Confetti

Ingredients:

- 1½ cups of vegetable stock or chicken stock (homemade is best)
- 1 cup quinoa, thoroughly rinsed and drained
- ½ teaspoon black pepper
- salt to taste, or a dash of soy sauce
- 1 cup mixed, diced vegetables such as carrots, peas, corn, green beans, red pepper etc (fresh cooked or frozen)

*This is a really flexible recipe. With quinoa the sky is the limit...almost! Add chopped avocado, cucumber, tomato, raisins, pineapple, olives, meat etc.

Directions:

1. *Place the stock into a medium saucepan and bring to the boil.*
2. *Stir in the rinsed quinoa, salt, and pepper.*
3. *Reduce heat to low and cover the pot with lid.*
4. *Cook for about 15 min until liquid has evaporated and the quinoa is tender.*
5. *Stir in veggies with a fork.*
6. *Place lid back on quinoa. The heat from the quinoa will cook the vegetables.*
7. *Put into an airtight container and refrigerate. Great in a chilled lunch box with cold meat and fruit.*

ANTS ON A LOG

Ingredients:

- 2 celery stalks
- 4 Tbsp your favorite Paleo friendly nut butter (almond butter or cashew butter are just fine)
- 2 Tbsp raisin (can also use other dried berries like black currants etc)

Directions:

1. *Cut the celery in thumb sized pieces.*
2. *Spread nut butter on each stalk.*
3. *Top with raisins or other dried berries of your choice.*

*Place in a lunchbox container so the peanut butter doesn't go everywhere.

BERRY LA DI DA FRUIT SALAD

Ingredients:

- 1 cup strawberries
- 1/2 cup blueberries
- 1 cup blackberries or boysenberries
- 1 cup kiwi fruit
- 1 banana (optional)
- 1/2 apricot or mango
- squeeze of lemon juice (helps keep fruit fresh for longer)

dollop of coconut cream and 1 apple if having for lunch at home

Directions:

1. *Pure and simple - Slice fruit up into bite sized pieces, add a sprig of mint and pop into lunch box containers. Add a dollop of coconut cream if suitable.*

APPLE CIDER COLESLAW

Ingredients:

- 1 small green or red cabbage (can use a mix of both)
- 1 carrot
- 2 Tbsp apple cider vinegar
- 1 Tbsp olive oil
- 1 tsp raw honey
- ¼ tsp ground mustard seed
- ¼ tsp cumin seed, ground
- ¼ tsp celery seed
- salt and black pepper to taste

Directions:

1. *Finely shred cabbage and carrot. Mix them both in a large bowl.*
2. *In another bowl, whisk together all other ingredients to create the dressing.*

3. *Add the dressing to the coleslaw. Mix it well together.*

Enjoy with a can of sardines or cold meat!

QUICK QUINOA SALAD

Ingredients:

- 3/4 cup water
- 1 tsp olive oil
- 1/2 cup quinoa, uncooked and rinsed
- 1/2 Spanish red onion, finely chopped (spring onions work too)
- 1/4 cup red capsicum pepper, diced
- 1/4 tsp mild curry powder
- juice from 1/2 a lime (sometimes I use lemon)
- 1/2 cup mixed diced vegetables such as carrot, peas and tomato
- 1/2 cup sultanas or currants (optional)
- 1 chopped avocado (optional)
- about 1 - 2 Tbsp of chopped fresh herbs such as basil, parsley, chives or cilantro
- salt and ground black pepper to taste

Directions:

1. *Cook the quinoa as per directions: bring water to the boil and pour in quinoa and oil. Reduce heat to a simmer and boil for about 15 mins or until water has been absorbed.*
2. *Place the cooked quinoa into a bowl, and chill in refrigerator until cold, around 20 mins.*
3. *Remove quinoa from fridge and stir in all the other ingredients.*
4. *Season to taste with salt and pepper.*
5. *Chill before serving.*

This is a filling and nutritious cold lunch or lunch box meal. Play around with the ingredients. Sometimes dried apricot is nice for a change. If the kids don't like something, leave it out.

ASPARAGUS, TOMATO AND ROCKET SALAD

Ingredients:

- 2 cups arugula, or rocket, or mixed leafy green salad leaves
- 1 cup tomatoes, cut in big pieces
- ½ cup asparagus
- 2 Tbsp avocado oil
- 2 Tbsp balsamic vinaigrette
- salt and black pepper to taste

  *If feeling extravagant wrap asparagus with ham or crispy fried bacon strips

Directions:

1. *Mix together arugula leaves, asparagus and tomatoes.*
2. *In a small bowl combine the avocado oil, balsamic vinaigrette, salt and pepper. Sprinkle it over the salad.*
3. *Pack it up and enjoy!*

COCONUT CREAM DIP

Ingredients:

- 1 cup coconut oil
- 1 cup coconut or cow's milk
- 1 cup agave nectar or honey
- 1 Tbsp water
- 5 tsp arrowroot powder
- a pinch of salt

Directions:

1. *In a saucepan simmer coconut milk, agave nectar and salt for 10 minutes.*
2. *Mix arrowroot powder and water in a small bowl until they form a paste.*
3. *Add this mixture in the sauce pan. Mix well and bring the mixture to boil for a short amount of time so it would get shiny.*

4. *Remove the pot from heat and gradually blend in the coconut oil. Let it cool down.*
5. *Place the pot in refrigerator for 2 hours and then blend again to so the texture gets airy.*
6. *Spread this cream on cakes, muffins or use it as a dip for fruit.*

TAHINI HUMMUS

Ingredients:

- 1 cauliflower head
- 1/2 cup Tahini (sesame paste)
- juice of 1 lemon
- 4 cloves garlic, smashed into a paste
- 4 Tbsp olive oil
- 2 tsp cumin, ground
- paprika powder and cayenne pepper to taste if desired
- salt and black pepper to taste

Directions:

1. *Preheat oven to 350 F (180 C)*
2. *Cut the cauliflower in small pieces.*
3. *In a bowl mix it together with olive oil, cumin, salt and pepper.*
4. *Place the spiced cauliflower to rimmed baking sheet and spread it out evenly.*
5. *Bake until the cauliflower is golden brown and tender (for 25-30 minutes). Stir occasionally.*
6. *Mix the roasted cauliflower with Tahiti, garlic, lemon juice in the food processor and blend until smooth.*
7. *Place hummus in a bowl and sprinkle with paprika for a dash of color.*
8. *Place in airtight lunch containers and refrigerate.*

* Great with favorite crackers, carrot sticks etc.

EASY GUACAMOLE DIP

Ingredients:

- 2 ripe avocados
- 2 tomatoes
- 2 garlic cloves, minced
- ½ cup fresh coriander or cilantro, finely chopped
- 1 Tbsp lime juice
- salt and pepper to taste

Directions:

1. *Make sure that the avocados are ripe. Peel them, cut in halves and place the pulps in a bowl.*
2. *Blanche tomatoes. Bring water to boil, put the tomatoes in the water for a minute, take them out and peel.*
3. *Put all the ingredients in the bowl and mash with a fork to create guacamole.* **If you like it super smooth or have some fussy eaters, use a blender.** *Accompany with crackers, flat bread, celery and carrot sticks. Top with herbs if desired.*

APPLE PIE BALLS

These are perfect for kids lunch box treats or anytime treats for that matter! You can use stewed apple, but it must be quite a "dry" mix. Get the kids help rolling the little apple pies in the coconut.

Ingredients:

- 1 cup cinnamon apple chips (store bought or homemade)
- 1 cup cooked or canned apple (not too wet)
- 1 cup coconut flakes
- 1 cup soft dates (prunes work too)
- 3/4 cup raisins or sultanas

* Optionally stealth bomb in a tsp of chia seeds and 1/4 cup oats.

Directions:

1. Place everything except raisins in a food processor and process about 2 minutes or until mixture would form a ball if moulded in your hand.
2. The apple chips should be 1/2 cm shards. Add raisins and blend (use pulse button) a few more times to get the correct consistency. If you prefer a smoother mix; simply process all ingredients together at start (including raisins).
3. Form into small sized balls. You may roll them in extra coconut flakes if dough is too sticky. (my kids were a little heavy on the coconut) Great for the lunch box!

CHOCOLATE & APRICOT BON BONS

Ingredients:

- 1 cup raw cashew nuts (can use walnuts or almonds)
- 1 cup dried apricots
- 8 large dates, pitted
- 4 Tbsp small dark chocolate chips
- 2 tsp chia seeds (optional)
- 4 Tbsp good quality cocoa powder (can mix with Milo)

Directions:

1. Put the dates, apricots and cashews in food processor and blend until smooth.
2. Add the chocolate chips and pulse just a bit to mix them in.
3. Create bonbons out of the mixture.
4. Coat each bonbon lightly in cocoa powder.
*The kids always love helping with this recipe. Stealth bomb in some ground pumpkin seeds too. What kids don't like these in the lunch box!!

CAROUSEL CARAMEL DIP

Ingredients:

- 1 cup dates, pitted
- 1 cup raw almonds (or cashews, or other nuts you like)
- 1/4 cup almond or regular milk
- 1 Tbsp coconut oil
- 1 tsp lemon juice
- 1 tsp vanilla extract
- a pinch of salt

Directions:

1. Soak the dates for 2 to 3 hours until they become soft.
2. Place all ingredients in the blender and blend until the texture is creamy. Serve in a pretty carousel shape in the lunchbox or plate with sliced fruit for dipping.

SWEET CHILI DIP

Ingredients:

- 1 small red chili, minced finely
- 2 garlic cloves, minced
- 5 Tbsp white wine vinegar
- 2 Tbsp raw honey
- 1 tsp arrowroot powder
- 1 tsp ginger, grated
- ¼ tsp cayenne pepper
- a pinch of salt

Directions:

1. Mince the garlic and grate the ginger. Finely mince the chili.
2. Combine the chili, garlic, ginger, vinegar, honey, arrowroot powder, ginger, cayenne pepper and arrowroot in a small saucepan. Mix them well.
3. Cook for a minute until the sauce thickens.
4. This dip tastes great with meat, fish or vegetables.

CUCUMBER DIP

Ingredients:

- 2 small Lebanese cucumbers (1/2 continental cucumber is okay too)
- 1 cup coconut cream
- 1 tsp salt
- 1/2 tsp fresh basil mint if you can get it.
- juice of a lemon

Directions:

Blend all ingredients together in a food processor or blender. Cover and place in fridge until you need it. Goes well with meats and breads.

ON THE GO SNACK PACK

Ingredients:

- 1 cup almonds
- 1/2 cup raw pumpkin seeds
- 1/2 cup raisins
- 1/2 cup dried cranberries, mango or other desired fruit
- 1/2 cup dark chocolate chips or similar quality chocolate pieces

*Use a mix up of what you have on hand in the pantry. If I shop at the market and find a bargain on some dried fruit, that features as a base for my mixes. Pine nuts, sunflower seeds are often on my list too. Just use what you have at the time.

Directions:

1. *Combine all ingredients.*
2. *Put them in an air tight container ready for the lunch box.*

   *Fruit and nut mixes are high energy making them great for busy kids at school keeping their metabolic rate ticking over.

Self Rising Flour Recipe

Need Self Rising Flour?

Even though this tip relates to wheat flour, it may be helpful to some. It is annoying when you need self raising flour in a recipe, but don't have any in the pantry. Here is how to make your own self-rising flour: **In a small bowl mix 1 cup of all-purpose flour,1 1/4 teaspoons of baking powder and 1/4 teaspoon of salt.**

GLUTEN FREE CORN DOG MUFFINS

Ingredients:

- 1 1/2 cups almond meal
- 1/2 tsp baking soda
- 1/2 tsp salt
- 1/4 tsp garlic flakes
- 1/3 cup raw honey
- 4 eggs
- 3 uncured organic hotdogs, roughly chopped (or desired allergy friendly hotdog or natural Chorizo sausage if you can find them organic and uncured) This depends on your needs.
  *cheese sprinkled on top is optional, depending on your child's needs.

Directions:

1. *Preheat oven to 350°F (180°C)*
2. Combine all ingredients in your electric mixer or food processor until there are no lumps.
3. *Fold in the chopped hotdogs or Chorizo pieces. (If desired you can just put one larger piece in the middle last)*
4. *Pour into a greased or lined muffin tins.*
5. *Cook for about 25 to 30 mins. Freeze if desired, a real favorite!*

GLUTEN FREE GRANOLA

Ingredients:

- 3 cups assorted nuts & seeds (almonds, walnuts, sunflower seeds, etc)
- 1 cup dried or fresh cranberries, or other desired dried fruits
- 2 cups shredded coconut (unsweetened)
- 1/4 cup coconut or olive oil
- 1/2 cup sunflower seed butter
- 1/4 - 1/2 cup honey or maple syrup
- 1/4 tsp vanilla extract
- 1/2 tsp salt
- 1 tsp cinnamon

* Granola or healthy bars are always good in the lunch box. They are flexible with ingredients. Don't be afraid to use what you have in the pantry to mix things up!

Directions:

1. Line a baking dish / tray with baking paper and set aside.
2. Combine nuts & seeds into large bowl
3. Remove 1 cup of nuts & seeds mix and chop into small pieces
4. Place remaining 2 cups of nuts & seeds in blender and pulse till chopped quite finely – You should end up with a good mix of small and fine pieces
5. Return nuts & seeds to mixing bowl. Stir in dried cranberries and add coconut. Stir well combining contents together
6. Place a small saucepan on a low-med flame and add coconut oil, sunflower seed butter & honey, vanilla, salt & cinnamon to cook. Stir until mixture bubbles and then remove from heat
7. Pour hot liquid mixture over nut mixture, stirring to combine. Mix well.
8. Pour the combined nuts-and-honey mixture into prepared dish / tray and press together using wet hands or spoon pressing firmly to ensure ingredients are well packed together.
9. Leave mixture to sit for 2 hours, cover and then place in freezer for

at least 1 hour
10. *Remove from freezer and cut into chunk sized pieces or muesli bars slices with a very sharp knife.*

Always perfect for the lunch box.

MINI MEDITERRANEAN TARTS

You can divide this recipe into small tarts or 1 larger tart. The boys love this one! Go easy on the tomato and olives if you like.

Tart Base Ingredients:

- 1/4 cup of olive oil or coconut oil
- 2 eggs, beaten
- 2 1/2 cups almond flour (approx. - just till the dough comes together)
- 1/2 tsp raw salt

Tart Base Directions:

Preheat oven to 350* or 180° C. Combine eggs and olive oil until well-blended. Stir in the almond flour and salt and mix until a dough forms. Grease a pie plate, or mini tart molds and press dough into the bottom and a little way up the sides, into an even layer. Prick dough all over with a fork. Bake for 5 - 10 minutes and set aside.

Tart Ingredients:

- 5 beaten eggs
- 1/2 cup coconut or milk you prefer (cream works too)
- 1/4 tsp ground black pepper (less if you prefer)
- 1 diced large onion
- about 1/2 tsp of salt to taste (optional, as the sardines may add a saltiness)
- 1/2 tsp garlic powder or flakes (optional, I like using flakes)
- 1 can natural sardines, drained well
- 1/2 cup black Spanish olives, pitted (olives with a mild flavor are best)
- 1/2 cup cherry tomatoes or sun dried tomatoes, sliced

- 1/2 cup zucchini, sliced (optional)

Sometimes I add chopped kale or broccoli florets and/or mushrooms to this tart instead of sardines.

Tart Directions:

1. Combine eggs, milk and pepper in a large bowl and set aside.
2. Cook onion over medium heat until light brown, then add garlic (and zucchini if using) and cook for a few more minutes.
3. Stir onion and garlic into the egg mixture. Arrange the sardines evenly over the crust, then the sliced tomato and olives.
4. Pour the egg mix over the top and place back in the oven to bake for a further 25 minutes or until the center is firm. About 10 - 15 mins for small tarts. It will set slightly more on standing. Top with more tomato and olive if desired.
*Wonderful power food packed with nutrition for the lunch box!

CARROT AND APPLE MUFFINS

If an egg allergy is a concern, try using Ener-G egg replacer as directed.

- 2 1/2 cups almond flour
- 1 Tbsp cinnamon
- 1/2 tsp raw salt
- 2 tsp baking soda
- 1 1/2 - 2 cups fresh carrots, peeled and grated
- 1 apple, peeled, cored and grated (any type)
- 3/4 cup shredded coconut
- 3/4 cup sultanas or chopped prunes (raisins or dried apricots are good too)
- 3 large eggs
- 1/2 cup olive oil
- 2 Tbsp raw honey or maple syrup
- 1 tsp vanilla extract

Directions:

1. *Preheat oven to 350°F (180°C)*
2. *Combine almond flour, cinnamon, salt and baking soda in a large bowl.*
3. *Add the grated carrot, apple, coconut and sultanas and combine well.*
4. *In another smaller bowl, whisk together the eggs, olive oil, vanilla and honey and oil well.*
5. *Pour the wet mixture into the dry ingredients and fold in gently.*
6. *Spoon the mixture into a lined or greased muffin pan.*
7. *Place on the top or middle rack of your oven and cook for about 35 - 40 minutes until a skewer comes out clean.*
8. *Cool in the pan for 5 minutes and then place on rack to cool.*

GLUTEN FREE BROWNIES

Ingredients:

- 1 cup applesauce (can use one ripe banana or cooked pumpkin puree)
- 1/2 cup coconut flour
- 1/2 cup coconut oil
- 1/2 cup cocoa powder
- 1/2 cup strong good quality coffee
- 10 dates, pitted (dates are a sweetener, so if you can cut down to 7 - 8 if desired)
- 3 eggs or Ener-G egg replacer
- 2 tsp vanilla extract
- 1 tsp baking soda
- pinch of salt

*Stealth bomber in 1 tsp pumpkin and/or sunflower seeds and 1/2 cup grated zucchini.

Directions:

1. *Preheat oven to 350°F (180°C)*
2. *Place the dates in a food processor and blend until smooth.*
3. *Add applesauce and continue to blend until it is well mixed with the dates.*

4. *Mix in the eggs, vanilla, coconut oil and coffee until the texture is smooth.*
5. *In a separate bowl combine coconut flour, cocoa powder, baking soda and salt.*
6. *Slowly add the dry ingredients to the mixture in the food processor and mix them well together on low speed until smooth.*
7. *Grease a baking pan with coconut oil and pour in the batter, even it out with a spatula.*
8. *Bake the brownies for 35 minutes.*
9. *Let the cake cool down. Cut in squares suitable for the lunch box.*

NUTTY BANANA MUFFINS

Not for anyone concerned about nut or egg allergies, beware.

Ingredients:

- 2 medium - large ripe bananas, mashed (about 1 cup)
- 2 eggs
- 1 tsp vanilla extract
- 1/3 cup coconut oil, melted or olive oil
- 1 Tbsp maple syrup or honey
- 1/3 cup coconut flour
- 1/4 tsp salt
- 1/2 tsp baking soda
- 1/4 tsp ground cinnamon
- 1/3 cup dark 85% cacao chocolate (optional, can use fruit or nuts instead)

*Use extra raw walnuts, almonds, pecans, macadamia or cashew nuts to garnish by sprinkling on top before muffins go in the oven.

Directions:

1. *Preheat oven to 350 F (180C) and prepare a 12 muffin lined tin.*

2. *In a large bowl add bananas and blend using a hand mixer until completely mashed. Add eggs, vanilla, oil, and syrup. Use a hand mixer to mix everything together, about 1 minute.*

3. *Add coconut flour, baking soda, salt, and cinnamon to the wet ingredients and mix again using hand mixer until everything is incorporated.*

4. *Stir in broken up chocolate pieces or any other nuts or fruits if using.*

5. *Scoop batter evenly into muffin tin.*

6. *Bake 20 to 25 minutes until light golden and a toothpick comes out clean.*

7. *Allow muffins to cool for 5 minutes. Remove from pan.*

8. *Store muffins in an airtight container for 2-3 days. They can keep longer in refrigerator or even longer in the freezer.*

Gluten Free Savoury Muffins

Ingredients:

- 1/2 cup coconut flour
- 1/2 tsp salt
- 4 large eggs at room temperature
- 2 1/2 Tbsp unsweetened applesauce
- 2 tsp apple cider vinegar
- 2 1/2 Tbsp raw honey that has been warmed
- 1/2 cup coconut oil, also warmed

Directions:

* Don't over mix or they will be tough and not rise well!

1.*Preheat oven to 350 F (180C).*

2. *Stir the coconut flour and salt together in a mixing bowl until well combined, with no clumps. Set aside.*

3. *Place the eggs, applesauce and vinegar into a blender or food processor and mix for about 5 seconds only.*

4. *Keep the blender on and now slowly add in the honey that has been warmed and the coconut oil, blending for another few seconds until*

combined. Add the dry ingredients and blend until combined, but only about 10 seconds.
5. Pour in to a lined muffin tin (about 3/4 full) Should get about 10 - 12 small muffins.
6. Bake for about 20-25 minutes or until a skewer comes out clean. Allow to cool for 10 minutes before removing from the muffin tray.

*These are wonderful in the lunch box with cold meats and salads.

CHOCOLATE ZUCCHINI BAR

Ingredients:

- 1/2 cup natural butter
- 1 1/2 cups sugar, sweetness substitute of choice or about 10 dates (natural sweetener)
- 1/2 cup vegetable oil
- 2 eggs or Ener-G egg replacer
- 1 tsp vanilla extract
- 1/2 tsp salt
- 2 1/2 cups all-purpose flour (or gluten free alternative)
- 4 Tbs good quality cocoa powder
- 1 tsp baking soda
- 1/2 cup sour milk, or coconut milk (can sour with a few drops of vinegar)
- 1/2 cup choc chips
- 1 1/2 cups grated zucchini

*Stealth bomber in about 1 Tbsp pumpkin seeds or sunflower seeds and 1 tsp of cinnamon too!

Directions:

1. *Preheat the oven to 325 F (170 C)*
2. *Cream the butter, sugar, oil, eggs, and vanilla together. Beat well.*
3. *Mix the flour, salt, cocoa, and baking soda together. Add dry ingredients to first mixture alternately with sour milk. Fold in zucchini and choc chips.*

4. *Bake in a sandwich shaped pan for about 30 - 35 mins or until done. Lunch box heaven for most kids!*

DATE CAROB TRUFFLES

Another special treat to keep the kids active throughout the day at school. Remember, you don't want to fill the lunch box with foods such as this alone. However, if these lunch box snacks are homemade you know what goes in them...and that means no added preservatives and artificial flavorings. Hooray to that!

Ingredients:

- 1 cup dates, pitted
- 1/2 cup butter
- 4 Tbsp coconut shreds
- 1 tsp chia seeds
- 2 Tbsp carob or cocoa powder
- 1 Tbsp coconut butter
- 1 tsp chocolate extract

*Stealth bomber in some pumpkin seeds, crushed nuts or diced prunes, dates or dried apricots.
Let the kids help with this one!

Directions:

1. *Boil water in a saucepan. Carefully throw in dates and bring to boil. Boil until soft.*
2. *Remove the dates from water and mash them with a potato masher.*
3. *Add almond butter, coconut butter, carob powder and chocolate extract to the dates. Combine until smooth.*
4. *Create small balls. Toss them in coconut shreds.*
5. *Freeze the truffles for a bit until they get firm.*

HOMEMADE KETCHUP

Ingredients:

- 5 lbs (2.250 kg) tomatoes
- 1/2 cup vinegar (apple cider vinegar okay)
- 1/4 cup onions, finely chopped
- 1 clove garlic, minced
  salt, black pepper, cayenne pepper, basil and sugar or stevia to taste

Directions:

1. *Blanche tomatoes by dropping them in boiling water for a minute. This should make them easy to peel. Carefully take them out of the boiling water and peel their skins off.*
2. *Cut the tomatoes in half, then scoop out the seeds with a spoon.*
3. *Put the tomatoes in a large pot for simmering. Add all the spice and vinegar. Simmer for 20-30 minutes.*
4. *Run the tomato mixture through a food mill or sieve.*
5. *Put your homemade ketchup in sanitized jars.*

Natural is best if you have time to manage it, especially around tomato growing season!

LITTLE LUNCHBOX MEATBALLS

This is a flexible recipe. Throw in some finely chopped kale, spinach, carrot or garlic if you like!

Ingredients:

- 2lbs (910g) grass-fed ground beef
- 15 oz (425g) homemade or natural tomato ketchup
- 6 oz (170g) tomato paste
- 1/4 cup almond meal (using diced bread will also make the meatballs tender)
- 1/4 cup natural beef stock
- 1/4 cup honey or maple syrup

- 1 onion, finely diced
- 1 egg
- 1 garlic clove, finely minced
- 1/4 tsp mild chili powder or natural BBQ seasoning (optional)
- 2 tsp Worcestershire sauce(can use gluten free)
- salt and ground black pepper to taste
- 1 tsp sesame seeds - optional
- 2 - 3 Tbsp olive or coconut oil for frying.

Directions:

1. Combine all the ingredients in a mixing bowl except the oil. (I use an electric mixer with the dough hooks on for mixing)
2. Mix well till well combined.
3. Wet hands and create small meatballs of an even size, ideal for the lunch box.
4. Heat the oil to medium high in a skillet and brown the meatballs on all sides by tossing occasionally.

*Cool and keep adequately chilled, serving with a dip. Use some toothpicks and add some other salad foods for a decorative presentation.

TASTY RAISIN MEATBALLS

For a special surprise, wrap in edible leaves!

Ingredients:

- 1 1/2 lbs (700g) lean beef mince
- 1/2 cup stale bread (optional, but this helps to make a more tender mix)
- 1 egg (optional due to allergies. If you don't use, cut bread down to just under 1/2 cup to balance wet & dry)
- 3 1/2 Tbsp of your favorite natural BBQ or chili sauce
- 2/3 cup blanched almonds, toasted in the over or on the stove top (optional)
- 2/3 cup dried raisins, sultanas or currants (can experiment with apricots too)

- 1 tsp freshly grated or dried garlic flakes
- 1/2 tsp ground black pepper
- 2 tsp raw salt

*Stealth bomber in some fresh finely chopped herbs from the garden. I like using parsley, basil, rosemary or chives.

Directions:

1. Reduce almonds into crumbs using a food processor (or blender)
2. Combine all ingredients either by hand or with (dough) electric mixer. **Make sure to "knead" the mixture** *for a few minutes to bind everything together properly and tenderize it.*
3. Wet your hands, roll the meat mixture into smallish balls the size of a whole walnut shell.
4. Heat the same frying pan to medium high, add some oil and place meatballs in. I usually cook about 6 at a time. Brown the first side of the meatballs, then reduce the heat down to medium and fry for about 3-4 minutes. Keep turning so all sides are cooked. (Should be cooked in about 10 - 15 minutes)
5. Remove from the pan and top with your favorite sauce or herbs and serve with salad or vegetables. Depending on the size you make the cooking time will vary slightly. Another option if you have the oven going is to pop them in there to finish cooking, Makes about a dozen meatballs.

Serve for lunch with a favorite sauce, or pop into a chilled lunch box and have separate sauce, salad and bread or roll.

PERFECT PUMPKIN PIE

Ingredients:

Filling

- 2 cups pumpkin purée
- 1 cup full fat cows milk or coconut milk
- 1/2 cup maple syrup
- 1/2 cup raw cashew nuts
- 3 eggs or Ener-G egg replacer
- 1 ripe avocado
- 1 tsp cinnamon
- pinch of salt

Crust

- 2 cups all purpose or almond flour
- 1 egg
- 2 Tbsp olive or coconut oil
- pinch of salt

Directions: *Preheat the oven to 350° F (180° C).*

Filling

1. *Place the cashew nuts in a food processor and blend until the texture is rough.*
2. *Peel the avocado, remove the core and add it to the cashew nuts.*
3. *Blend them together until the mixture is smooth.*
4. *Repeat these steps with pumpkin, then coconut milk, then all other ingredients. Mix thoroughly.*

Crust

1. *Form dough by placing all ingredients in the food processor and blending well.*
2. *Grease a pie pan and stretch the dough over it.*
3. *Pour in the filling, and bake the pie for 60 minutes.*

OMG OMELET ROLL

Ingredients:

- 2 eggs
- 1 spring onion, thinly sliced
- 4 Tbsp fully cooked lean ham, finely chopped
- 1 Tbsp almond milk
- 1 Tbsp sweet red capsicum pepper, finely diced or minced (I often use mushrooms or a mix of both)
- 1 Tbsp olive oil
- salt and black pepper to taste

Directions:

1. *In a small bowl whisk the eggs together with milk salt and black pepper. Then add the ham and red pepper. Mix well.*
2. *Heat a tablespoon of olive oil in skillet. Pour the egg mixture in.*
3. *Fry from one or both sides. Roll before serving.*
4. *Cut the omelet roll in small pieces so it will fit your lunchbox. Enjoy!*

EASY CRUSTLESS POPEYE QUICHE

This is really like an omelet made in the oven, the eggs make the mix "set". Grease the pan well.

Ingredients:

- 10 large eggs or Ener-G egg replacer
- 2 tsp olive oil or similar
- 1 onion, minced or finely diced
- 16 oz (450g) spinach, chopped (finely for fussy eaters)
- 1/2 cup sliced mushrooms
- 1 cup coconut cream, or milk (any cream of milk works, but for a richer flavor, use full pastured cream)
- salt and pepper to taste
- Can sprinkle with your favorite cheese or Paleo friendly alternative if desired.

* Optionally I add 2 rashers of crispy fried (diced) bacon pieces. My sons love this!

Directions:

1. *Preheat oven to 350° F (180° C).*
2. *Chop the spinach, onion and slice the mushrooms.*
3. *Fry in oil till golden.*
4. *In a bowl beat together eggs with cream or milk.*
5. *Grease a glass pan or similar.*
6. *Place all the fried ingredients into the pan. Pour the egg and milk mixture over the top.*
7. *Bake for around 25 - 30 minutes, or until egg almost looks set.*
8. *Allow to cool for about 3 mins to set.*

*May serve hot for lunch or slice into lunch box sizes and serve cold.

Homemade Mayonnaise

Ingredients:

- 1¼ cup light olive oil
- 1 egg
- 2 Tbsp lemon juice
- ½ tsp dry mustard
- salt to taste

Directions:

1. *Blend the egg and lemon juice in a blender or food processor.*
2. *Add the other ingredients except the oil and mix them well.*
3. ***Very slowly drizzle in the olive oil while continually whisking. The trick here is to be very slow** otherwise the mixture will be more like salad dressing than mayonnaise.*

TIP: If you separate the egg and add half a tsp of water to the yolk before drizzling in the oil, this helps create a stronger and more stable mayonnaise.

BAKED APPLE BEAUTIES

Ingredients:

- 4 large apples
- 1 cup raisins or sultanas
- ½ cup blanched almond flour or all purpose flour
- 4 Tbsp walnuts, finely chopped
- 4 Tbsp maple syrup or honey
- 3 Tbsp cinnamon, ground

Directions:

1. *Preheat the oven to 350° F (180° C)*
2. *Cut the apple tops off and remove the cores without damaging the bottoms.*
3. *In a small bowl mix together almond flour, maple syrup and almond flour. Mix well, then stir in raisins and walnuts*
4. *Stuff each apple with the mixture.*
5. *Bake for 30 minutes, then cover with aluminum foil and continue cooking for 10 more minutes.*

*Wrap in aluminum foil to keep together when you pack these beauties up.

PUMPKIN BANANA BREAD

This recipe can take a little experimentation depending on your oven and quality of ingredients.

Ingredients:

- 1/2 cup coconut flour
- 1/2 cup almond flour
- 1/2 cup pumpkin puree
- 1/2 cup ripe banana, pureed
- 1/2 cup pecans, finely chopped (or ground for fussy eaters)
- 1/2 cup almond butter
- 1/4 cup raw honey
- 4 eggs

- 1 tsp baking soda
- 1/2 tsp vanilla extract
- 1/2 tsp salt

Directions:

1. *Preheat oven to 350° F (180° C)*
2. *In a large bowl mix together coconut flour, almond flour, baking soda and salt.*
3. *In another bowl combine the eggs, pumpkin puree, banana puree, almond butter, honey and vanilla extract. Mix all these wet ingredients well together until the texture becomes smooth.*
4. *Pour the liquid ingredients into the dry ingredients and add the pecans. Stir everything together until they are well combined.*
5. *Grease a loaf pan. Pour the batter in it and put it in the oven for about 45 minutes or until a toothpick comes out clean when picked.*
6. *This pumpkin banana bread tastes great on its own in the lunch box, or can also be eaten with a jam or coconut cream for lunches.*

SUPER CHILI BEEF LUNCH

Ingredients:

- 2 Tbsp coconut oil
- 1 diced onion
- 6 stalks of celery (diced)
- 4 garlic cloves (minced)
- 3 1/2 pounds (about 1.3kg) ground beef
- 4 tsp ground cumin
- 1 tsp mild chilli powder (optional)
- 4 tsp oregano
- 2 x 12 oz (375g) jars of salsa or natural tomato puree
- 2 x 8 oz (250g) cans of diced tomatoes
- 4 tsp salt

* This is a powerhouse of goodness for lunches! I often add diced red peppers and carrots too. Use the stealth method; add about 1/2 cup pureed/blended spinach or kale. They won't even know it's in there!

Directions:

1. Using a large pot; fry onions, celery & garlic in coconut oil over med-high heat.
2. Cook for about 4 minutes adding beef and spices. Cook for further 5 minutes; stirring constantly.
3. Add tomatoes, salsa green chillies & salt. Simmer for about 1 hour.
*Serves a hungry family of 4 - 6 Great when you 4. are in need of a quick and easy recipe. I like to add a small bunch of chopped parsley at the end of cooking if it's growing in the garden.

*This beef recipe is a favorite in the kids lunch box if it can be heated. Mind you it's even okay cold! It's especially good for Paleo cave-kids!

MIDDLE EASTERN COUSCOUS

Quick, easy, non Paleo but satisfying! Similar to confetti. You can find couscous gluten free varieties in some supermarkets. This is flexible...sometimes I use seeds or shaved and roasted almonds, sometimes not. Change it up to keep it interesting!

Ingredients:

- 1 cup of cooked gluten free couscous
- 1 Tbsp pine nuts
- 1 Tbsp of pumpkin seeds
- 1 Tbsp olive oil
- 2 spring onions or red onion, chopped
- pinch of ground cumin seeds
- pinch star anise
- 1/2 clove of garlic, crushed optional
- 1/2 cup vegetable stock
- 2 tsp lemon juice
- 2 tomatoes, chopped into small pieces
- 1/4 cup cucumber, chopped into small pieces
- Chopped fresh herbs like parsley, basil or chives

Directions:

1. *Roast the pumpkin seeds and pine nuts on the stove top or in the oven for 5 min.*
2. *In oil gently fry the onions and garlic until soft. Stir in the cumin and cook for about 30 seconds.*
3. *Pour in the stock, lemon juice and bring to boil, then turn off heat.*
4. *Add the couscous, stirring briefly and then cover the pan with a lid or plate. Leave for 5 min until all the liquid is absorbed.*
5. *Tip the mixture into a bowl, separating it briefly so it doesn't all stick together in a lump.*
6. *Mix all the remaining ingredients into bowl and season with salt and pepper if you like.*
7. *Place into a container suitable for the lunchbox, with a chiller pack.*

EASY LUNCHBOX FRITTATA

Ingredients:

- 8 eggs
- salt, pepper and herbs to season
- 2 cups of chicken or bacon, chopped into pieces (optional)
- 2 cups of mixed vegetables, chopped (onion, mushroom, spinach, zucchini, bell pepper)

Directions:

1. *Preheat oven to 350F (180C)*
2. *Lightly grease 2 x medium pie plates / muffin tins / 8 individual ramekins*
3. *Whisk eggs with seasonings in a large bowl*
4. *Place chopped meat and vegetables evenly in base of prepared dishes*
5. *Pour egg mixture evenly over (the meat and) veggies*
6. *Bake about 35 – 40 minutes.*

Frittatas should have golden edges, firm to touch. Smaller Frittatas cook in about 15 mins. Do not overcook, they become quite rubbery!

*Experiment with your own tasty combinations for lunch box creations. You can use any meat, poultry or fish and vegetable combo making it a great way to use up leftovers!

ASPARAGUS IN A BLANKET

Ingredients:

- 1lb (450g) tender asparagus, trimmed
- 6 to 8 thin slices bacon, ham or prosciutto, sliced to wrap around asparagus
- 1 Tbsp olive oil
- salt and black pepper to taste

Directions:

1. *Preheat oven to to 400°F (200°C)*
2. *Place the asparagus on baking sheet. Sprinkle with olive oil, salt and pepper.*
3. *Roast the asparagus in oven for about 10 - 15 minutes. Let them cool down.*
4. *Wrap each asparagus in bacon or ham and secure with a toothpick if needed.*

*Great for lunches. The kids might like helping you wrap the asparagus up in their blankets.

GINGERED APPLESAUCE

Ingredients:

- 3lb (1350g) apples, cores removed
- 6 fresh apricots, pitted and chopped roughly
- 1 tsp ginger, grated
- ½ tsp vanilla extract
- Water for boiling

*Can add 1 tsp of cinnamon.

Directions:

1. *Peel and roughly chop the apples.*
2. *Boil water in a big pot. Put the apple pieces in there and cook for 30 minutes. Stir frequently.*

3. *When half an hour has passed, add the apricots and ginger. Cook 10 more minutes.*
4. *Remove the pot from the heat and stir in vanilla extract.*
5. *Put the fruit in a food processor and blend until smooth. Place in individual lunch containers.*

*This is a healthy lunch or brunch snack for kids and adults to enjoy. Great with other fruits or on it's own. Wonderful for when the kids arrive home from school hungry, just serve with yoghurt or ice cream.

GLUTEN FREE BREAD

I don't make breads much, so this recipe may take some practice as I have been told ingredient quality and oven temps can affect the result. Perhaps have some standby bread the first time you try it and adjust if needed!

Ingredients:

- 2 cups almond flour
- 1/2 tsp salt
- 1 tsp baking soda
- 1/3 cup + 1 Tbsp flaxseed meal
- 1/2 cup arrowroot powder
- 6 Tbs coconut oil
- 4 fresh eggs
- 1 tsp apple cider vinegar
- 1/2 cup coconut cream (can use natural butter)

* Stealth bomb with up to 1/4 cup of finely chopped nuts or seeds to this mix if desired.

Directions:

1. *Preheat the oven to 350° F or 180° C*
2. *In a large bowl, mix the flour, salt, baking soda, flaxseed meal and arrowroot powder.*
3. *Melt the butter in a small saucepan and allow it cool for about 5 minutes.*
4. *Whisk the coconut cream with the eggs, vinegar and cream.*

5. *With a rubber spatula or spoon, very gently mix wet and dry ingredients to form a batter.* **Don't over mix or the batter will get oily, dense and not rising properly.**
6. *Now pour the batter into a lined or greased 8½" x 4½" medium bread loaf pan. Sprinkle top with whole nuts or flax-seeds.*
7. *Place into the oven and bake until a wooden skewer comes out clean, about 25 minutes.*
8. *Cool thoroughly, then cut into slices and place into lunch box with cold meats.*

SESAME CRACKERS

Try poppy seeds if you like.

Ingredients:

- 3 cups almond flour
- 1 cup sesame seeds
- 2 eggs, whisked
- 2 Tbsp olive oil
- 1½ tsp salt

Directions:

1. *Preheat the oven to 350° F or 180° C*
2. *Mix all ingredients in a big bowl.*
3. *Line two large baking sheets with parchment paper. Place half of the dough right in the middle of each sheet. Place another piece of parchment paper over the dough mounds.*
4. *Evenly roll the dough between the parchment papers until it covers entire baking sheet. Do that for both baking sheets. Remove the parchment paper and cut the dough with a pizza cutter into small squares, or use a scone cutter or glass for circular biscuits.*
5. *Bake for 10-15 minutes or until golden brown.*

* A popular snack in the lunch box with dips and cold meats.

GLUTEN FREE RASPBERRY & ALMOND MUFFINS

If nut allergies are a problem, try the "Coconut Flour Cranberry Muffins" instead.

Ingredients:

- 1 cup almond flour
- 1 cup almond butter
- 1 cup fresh raspberries, or blueberries (sometimes I add jam if I don't have fresh fruits)
- 1/2 cup olive or coconut oil
- 1/4 cup raw honey
- 1/4 cup shaved almonds
- 3 eggs, whisked
- 1 tsp baking powder
- pinch of salt

Directions:

1. *Preheat oven to 350°F or 180°C.*
2. *In a medium size bowl mix together all dry ingredients: almond flour, baking powder and salt.*
3. *In another bowl combine almond butter, honey coconut oil and eggs.*
4. *Combine the dry and wet ingredients. Don't over mix!*
5. *Fold in raspberries.*
6. *Scoop the batter in slightly greased muffin cups (or use paper muffin liners). Cover each muffin with sliced almonds as decoration.*

* If using jam instead, fill muffin pan only half way up, then add jam, then put another spoonful of batter on the top. This makes a lovely "sauce" surprise when you bite into the cooked muffin.

Baby Spinach & Bacon Quiche

This is a flexible recipe. Sometimes I add small cauliflower or broccoli florets instead of spinach and bacon. Use herbs you have in the garden to sprinkle on top. My favorites are parsley and onion chives. Use mini quiche tins if you like.

Quiche Base Ingredients:

- 1/4 cup of olive oil
- 2 eggs, beaten
- 2 1/2 cups almond flour (approx. - just till the dough comes together)
- 1/2 tsp raw salt

Quiche Base Directions:

1. *Preheat oven to 350° or 180° C*
2. *Combine eggs and olive oil until well blended.*
3. *Stir in the almond flour and salt and mix until a dough forms.*
4. *Grease a pie plate or prepare mini quiche tins and press dough into the bottom and up the sides, into an even layer. Prick dough all over with a fork. Bake for 10 minutes and set aside.*

Quiche Ingredients:

- 5 beaten eggs
- 3/4 cup coconut cream (or cream you desire)
- 1/2 tsp black pepper (less if you prefer)
- salt to taste (optional, as the bacon will add a saltiness)
- 1 cup diced bacon or ham pieces (not too large or it will be hard to cut quiche)
- 1 diced onion
- 1/2 tsp garlic powder or flakes (optional)
- 2 cups baby spinach or kale leaves (can use cooked and chopped spinach pieces without stalks)

*Optionally, top with about 1/2 - 3/4 cup of your preferred cheese.

Quiche Directions:

1. Combine eggs, milk and pepper in a large bowl and set aside.
2. Cook bacon or ham and onion over medium heat until golden brown, then add garlic and spinach leaves last cooking for a few more minutes till all combined.
3. Stir onion/bacon/spinach mix into the egg mixture.
4. Pour into the crust. (Add grated cheese now if desired) Place back in the oven to bake for a further 25 minutes or until the center is firm. It will set slightly more on standing. Serve with a salad for lunch and leftovers can go in the chilled lunch box next day.

An old time favorite.

CORN DOGS

Ingredients:

- 12 oz (340g) cooked ham, ground
- 12 oz (340g) raw pork, ground
- 1/2 cup almond or gluten free flour
- 1/4 cup flax meal
- 1/2 cup onion, finely chopped
- 2 eggs, beaten or Ener-G egg replacer
- 2 Tbsp coconut milk or desired milk
- 1 tsp mustard
- salt and pepper to taste

*You can roll in almond meal before cooking for a change.

Directions:

1. *Combine both meats with eggs, almond flour, flax meal, onion, coconut milk, mustard, salt and pepper in a large bowl.*
2. *Shape the mixture into small corn dogs, around 20.*
3. *Cook in oven at 350° F or 180° C for 40 minutes or until done.*
4. *Place in lunch box after putting skewers through them.*

*The kids love eating from the sticks! Goes well with dips or mustard on the side.

BANANA NUT LOAF

I can still remember eating my mum's nut loaf when I was at school. Yum!

Ingredients:

- 1/2 cup raw walnuts, chopped (other preferred nuts are fine too)
- 2 large over ripe bananas, mashed
- 1/2 Tbs vanilla extract
- 3 large fresh eggs (or egg replacer)
- 1 Tbs raw honey or maple syrup
- 1/4 cup natural butter
- 2 cups blanched almond flour
- 1 tsp baking soda

(If you want, use a gluten free flour alternative instead)
Stealth bomber in 1/2 cup grated zucchini or carrot and 1 tsp chia seeds. Variations I use for this recipe include: 2 tsp flax-seeds or add apricots or grated carrot instead of banana. Depends on the mood and what's in the pantry! A very flexible recipe...get creative!

Directions:

1. *Heat the oven to 350 F or 180 C.*
2. *Line or grease a 7 x 3 loaf pan.*
3. *Put the walnuts, mashed bananas, vanilla, eggs, honey and butter into your food processor and pulse.*
4. *Gently pulse in the almond flour, baking soda and the salt.*
5. *Scoop the mixture into the loaf tin and bake for about 1 hour until a skewer comes out clean. Popular lunch fodder!*

SPICE GIRL WHOOPIE PIES

Ingredients:

- 2 cups almond flour or regular all purpose flour
- 1 cup of raw honey or maple syrup
- 2 eggs
- 1 Tbsp vanilla
- 1 Tbsp apple cider vinegar
- 1 tsp cinnamon
- 1 tsp dry ginger, ground
- 1/2 tsp baking soda
- 1/2 tsp allspice
- 1/2 tsp nutmeg
- 1/4 tsp cloves, ground
- pinch of salt

Creamy Vanilla Frosting (for one whoopie pie):

- 4 Tbsp natural butter
- 2 Tbsp raw honey
- 1/2 tsp vanilla

Directions:

1. *Preheat the oven to 350° F or 180° C*
2. *Mix together the flour, vanilla, cinnamon, ginger, baking soda, allspice, nutmeg, cloves and salt. In another bowl combine honey with eggs and apple cider vinegar.*
3. *Blend both of these mixes together.*
4. *Cover baking sheets with parchment paper. Put heaping tablespoons of dough on the sheet. Flatten them out to form a whoopie pie.*
5. *Bake for about 10-15 minutes or until hardened enough for toothpick to come out clean.*
6. *Meanwhile mix all the frosting ingredients together with a whisk.*
7. *Let the whoopie pies cool for a while. Take one pie, put the frosting on it and then place another pie on top of it.*

ALMOND FLOUR BROWNIES

Almond flour is a favorite as it is high in protein. Experiment with this one.

Ingredients:

- 1 cup almond flour or all purpose flour
- 1/2 cup coconut oil
- 4oz (115g) baking chocolate
- 7 dates
- 3 eggs
- 1/2 tsp baking soda
- 1/4 tsp vanilla stevia, or sweetener of your choice
- pinch of salt

* Stealth bomb in some chia seed, or finely chopped pumpkin seeds or dried fruits.

Directions:

1. *Preheat the oven to 350° F or 180° C*
2. *In a food processor mix together almond flour, salt and baking soda. Slowly add squares of dark chocolate until the texture is like coarse sand.*
3. *Add eggs, coconut oil and Stevia until the mixture is smooth.*
4. *Pour the mixture in a baking dish, smooth it out with a spatula.*
5. *Bake for roughly 20 minutes or until a toothpick comes out clean.*

*Lunch box favorite! Try using your preferred gluten free flour if you want.

ALLERGY FREE TORTILLAS

Ingredients:

- 1½ cup of full fat coconut milk
- 1/4 cup almond flour
- 1/4 cup coconut flour
- 1/4 cup flax meal
- 6 eggs (or try Ener-G egg replacer)
- 1/2 tsp baking powder
- 1/2 tsp salt
- olive or coconut oil for frying

Directions:

1. *Preheat a medium sized skillet on medium or low heat.*
2. *Mix all ingredients with a blender until smooth.*
3. *Coat the skillet with coconut oil. Pour batter into the skillet to create a thin tortilla. Cook on both sides. Repeat the same process with the remaining batter.*
4. *Put in lunchbox with your child's favorite filling. The options are endless – dips, fruit, berries, salad, meatballs, eggs and many more. Tasty!*

APPLE CINNAMON CHIPS

Ingredients:

- 2 large apples
- 2 cups apple juice
- 1 cinnamon stick

Directions:

1. *Preheat oven to 250°F (120°C).*
2. *In a pot combine apple juice and cinnamon stick. Bring it to boil.*
3. *Remove the apple cores and slice the apples crosswise to create chips.*

4. *Carefully put the apple slices in the boiling juice and cook for 5 minutes.*
5. *Take the apple slices out of the juice and place on a cloth. Pat dry.*
6. *Place the apple slices on a wire cooling rack placed on a baking sheet.*
7. *Bake the apple slices for 35-40 minutes until they dry completely.*
8. *Let them cool to go crispy.*

*These are great in the lunchbox or as on the go snacks! A wonderful alternative to greasy, salty potato chips.

MOROCCAN LAMB SKEWERS

The boys love this one for lunch or in the lunch box!

Ingredients:

- 2 lb (900g) of lean lamb fillets, cut into small cubes (beef or chicken works too)
- 1 medium red onion, finely chopped
- 3 Tbsp fresh parsley, minced
- 3 Tbsp fresh cilantro (coriander) minced
- 1 Tbsp olive oil
- 2 tsp paprika powder
- 1 tsp cumin, ground
- salt and black pepper to taste

Directions:

1. *Mix all ingredients in a bowl.*
2. *Cover the tray with a towel or plastic and let the lamb marinate for several hours in the refrigerator.*
3. *Put the meat pieces on skewers and grill on medium heat from all sides. Each side should take about 5 to 10 minutes.*

*Pack up in the lunch box with dips, be sure well chilled.

CORNFLAKE CHICKEN CORDON BLEU

If you want a more basic quick and easy recipe, check out the Quick Crunchy Chicken Strips.

Ingredients:

- 3 1/2 lbs or about 6 chicken breasts cut into 1/2 inch thick long slices
- 6 thin slices natural ham
- 6 thin slices Swiss cheese, or other cooking cheese you like
- 6 cups gluten free cornflakes, crushed fine to medium size
- 2 egg whites
- 1 1/2 tsp paprika or favorite seasoning

*Can add 1 cup chopped spinach leaves alternatively in layers if your child likes them. Paleo can omit cheese and add garlic if like.

Directions:

1. *Preheat the oven to 400F (205C)*
2. *Slice chicken fillets lengthwise in half. (you can use a mallet gently if you want to make them thin)*
3. *Top with 1 slice of ham and 1 of cheese.*
4. *Fold the fillet tightly in half lengthwise to cover the filling. Secure it with toothpicks. Repeat layering with all the chicken, ham and cheese.*
5. *Place the finely crushed cornflakes in a wide flat dish.*
6. *Place the whisked egg whites and paprika in a wide flat dish.*
7. *Coat each breast with the egg mix, then the cornflake mix and place on to a plate.*
8. *Once finished, transfer to a lined baking sheet. Bake until cooked through, around 30 minutes depending on the size of your chicken.*

Pack up in chilled lunch box with carrot, salad and fruits.

ALLERGY FREE CHOC CHIP COOKIES

If you want, make these larger for the lunch box.

Ingredients:

- 1 cup butter, softened
- 1 cup brown sugar
- 3/4 cup granulated sugar
- 1 1/2 tsp vanilla extract
- 2 eggs or Ener-G egg replacer
- 2 1/2 cups All Purpose or substitute flour of choice like rice gluten free flour
- 2 tsp xanthan gum
- 1 tsp gluten free baking powder
- 1/4 tsp salt
- 1 tsp baking soda
- 1 1/2 cups dark or light chocolate chips

*Stealth bomber in some seeds and chopped dried fruits or nuts of your choice.

Directions:

1. *Preheat the oven to 375F (190C)*
2. *On low speed in an electric mixer bowl, cream together the sugars, butter and vanilla for 3 minutes until mix turns lighter in color. Mix with spoon by hand if desired, until well blended. Beat in eggs on medium speed until light and fluffy.*
3. *In another bowl, mix together the flour, xanthan gum, baking powder, baking soda and salt.*
4. *Stir flour mixture into butter mixture. Stir in choc chips.*
5. *On lined cookie sheets, spoon mixture of dough in Tbsp size, a few inches apart to allow for spread.*
6. *Bake for about 8 minutes. The centre will still be slightly soft. Cool and store in an airtight container.*

Always a lunch box favorite!

QUICK CRUNCHY CHICKEN STRIPS

Ingredients:

- 2 - 3 chicken breasts, cut lengthways into strips of roughly even thickness
- 2 Tbsp gluten free all purpose flour (can use almond meal)
- 2 Tbsp crushed cornflakes
- 1 tsp salt or favorite seasoning
- 1/4 tsp ground black pepper
- 1/4 tsp paprika (optional)

* Stealth method in 1 tsp sesame seeds and 1 tsp dried mixed herbs

Directions:

1. *Preheat oven to 350F (180C)*
2. *Place all dry ingredients into a large plastic bag - give a shake to mix. Now add the cut up chicken strips, twist the top of the bag to seal, shake well till all are coated.*
3. *Place on a lined oven tray and cook for about 20 minutes until chicken is cooked. Easy!*

* Tasty with tomato ketchup, dips and salad or fruit for lunch time or at school. Make sure lunch box is well chilled.

MUESLI BAR MAGIC

A wonderful snack at home with milk or in the lunch box as the sweet treat. It's a flexible recipe, get creative!

Ingredients:

- 1/2 cup of natural butter
- 1/2 cup clear honey
- 1/4cup superfine caster sugar, or alternative natural sweetener such as Stevia
- 1/4 cup of mixed sunflower and sesame seeds
- 3 cups rolled oats (or 2 cups of crushed cornflakes for gluten free)

- 2 cups low sugar rice cereal
- 1 cup raisins or sultanas
- 1/2 cup chopped dried apricots, or dates, or cranberries, or cherries
- 1/2 cup desiccated coconut
- 1/4 cup pumpkin seeds
- 1/2 cup choc chips (optional)

*Stealthily add mixed nuts, Goji berries and chia seeds if desired.

Directions:

1. *Preheat oven to 350F (180C)*
2. *Line a baking tray with paper.*
3. *Combine honey, sugar and butter in a saucepan over a medium heat until butter melts and sugar dissolves.*
4. *Boil and cook for about 2 minutes until syrup thickens a little. Turn off the heat.*
5. *Combine all remaining ingredients in a large bowl.*
6. *Pour over the wet mix and stir all together to combine.*
7. *Spoon into the pan and press firmly down to make sure all the mixture will stick together.*
8. *Using a wet spoon, smooth out the top.*
9. *Bake in the oven for about 15 - 20 minutes or until golden.*
10. *Cool and then refrigerate for about 1 hour to firm up.*

* Great in any lunch box. A muesli bar with nutrition and an energizer.

NUT, EGG & GLUTEN FREE CHOC CHIP MUFFINS

Ingredients:

This is a very flexible recipe. If you can't find low allergy, gluten free all-purpose baking mix, use all-purpose flour. You can substitute applesauce/puree for mashed banana or use a combo of both. You can add less or more choc chips, or dried fruits. Instead of almond milk, you can use any milk. Seeds can be substituted for nuts if desired. You can add more or less sweetening. Just bear in mind the liquid/dry ratio.

Ingredients 1:

- 1 cup gluten-free, all-purpose baking mix (from Costco, health food shops or other supermarkets)
- 1 Tbsp sunflower seeds
- 1 Tbsp pumpkin seeds
- 1 cup choc chips (dark is good, depending on your child's taste buds)
- 1/2 Tbsp baking powder
- 1/2 tsp baking soda
- 1/4 tsp salt

*Stealth bomb in some chia seeds or cocoa nibs for older kids.

Ingredients 2: Mix in a separate bowl:

- 2 cups applesauce
- 1/4 cup brown sugar
- 3 Tbsp olive oil
- 1 Tbsp honey, maple syrup or Stevia
- 1/4 cup almond or coconut milk
- 1 tsp apple cider vinegar (or white)
- 1 tsp vanilla extract

Directions:

1. Preheat oven to 400F (205C)
2. Line or grease a 24 cup mini muffin tin or standard muffin tin with paper liners.
3. In a large bowl stir together the first lot of ingredients. Set aside.
4. In a medium sized bowl combine the second lot of ingredients.
5. Stir mix 2 into the flour mix 1 - ONLY until JUST combined, or muffins will be tough and won't rise properly.
6. Using a greased dessertspoon or tablespoon, scoop the batter out, and 3/4 fill the prepared muffin tins.
7. If you want to top with chocolate pieces or fruit, you can do it now.
8. Bake for 10 -12 minutes or until a skewer comes out clean.
9. Cool completely and pack for a super lunch snack.

ZUCCHINI & SALMON HASH BROWNS

Ingredients:

- 1 whole egg or Ener-G egg replacer
- 1 cup shredded zucchini
- 1 egg white (optional)
- 1 small can drained unsalted salmon (can use fresh, steamed)
- 2 tbs coconut flour
- 1/2 cup diced green/spring onion
- 1/4 tsp raw salt
- 1/4 tsp garlic flakes (optional)
- ground black pepper

*Stealth bomber mode coming up...finely sliced olives, broccoli, flaxseed oil, eggplant.

Directions:

*1. In a large bowl, place the shredded zucchini after **squeezing out all the excess water.***
2. Add all other ingredients and mix until thoroughly combined.
3. Heat a large non-stick skillet or pan sprayed with non-stick spray over medium-low heat.
4. With your hands, make small round patties out of the zucchini mixture and place into your pan.
5. Cook until golden brown, flipping halfway through.

Lunch box heaven. Can be eaten cold or hot. Makes about 6 "fat" hash browns.

CRANBERRY & WALNUT POWER BARS

Ingredients:

- 2 ½ cups blanched almonds or oats, or rice cereal
- 1 cup chopped or crushed walnuts (optional)
- 1 Tbsp coconut flour
- 1 Tbsp sunflower seeds
- 1 Tbsp pumpkin seeds
- 1/3 cup golden flax-meal (or similar)
- 1 cup dried cranberries or mix of other favorite berries
- 1 Tbsp honey, maple syrup (or stevia liquid to taste
- 1 tsp vanilla extract
- 1/2 cup shredded coconut
- 3 Tbsp water
- 1 Tbsp shredded coconut for top if desired (can add more)

Directions: This really is a flexible recipe. Be creative and use what you have on hand. Take out what you don't like!

1. *Place almonds, nuts, flour, seeds, flax, cherries, cranberries and vanilla into a blender or food processor. Pulse until well ground but not to a paste.*
2. *Now pulse in the water and shredded coconut until the mixture begins to form a ball. This is where you can change around and even out the wet/dry balance - add more water or coconut if needed.*
3. *Press into an 8 x 8 inch slice bar or pan and top into the fridge to firm. Now slice into bars. Makes about 14 bars.*

*Yet another one of those flexible lunch box recipes; be creative with fruit and nuts.

COCONUT FLOUR CRANBERRY MUFFINS

Ingredients:

- 6 eggs
- 4 Tbsp melted coconut butter or olive oil
- 1/2 tsp vanilla
- 4 Tbsp coconut milk
- 6 drops of Stevia liquid extract or similar sweetener (1/4 cup of coconut sugar can be also used, depending how sweet you like muffins)
- 1/2 tsp raw salt
- 1/2 tsp baking powder
- 1/2 cup sifted coconut flour
- 1 cup fresh cranberries or blueberries

Directions:

1. *Preheat the oven to 375F (190C)*
2. *In large bowl, mix the eggs, butter, vanilla, coconut milk, sugar or Stevia and salt.*
3. *In a separate small bowl combine sifted coconut flour and the baking powder.*
4. *Fold the dry mix into the batter gently, blending until there are no lumps.*
5. *Mix the cranberries in.*
6. *Pour batter into oiled or lined muffin tins and bake for about 15 minutes until a skewer comes out clean.*

* A lunchbox favorite!

EASY TUNA MORNAY MAGIC

Ingredients:

- 2 drained cans of tuna in olive oil or spring water
- 2 cups steamed cauliflower florets
- 1 chopped onion
- 2 large fresh beaten eggs, optional (these help thicken and set the casserole, but aren't necessary)
- 1 cup coconut milk
- 1/2 tsp garlic flakes (optional, I only add this if not using Brazil nut and garlic topping below)
- 1 1/2 Tbsp fresh or dried parsley or chives
- 1 Tbsp coconut flour
- salt and black pepper to taste
- 1/3 cup dairy free cheese substitute, optional (1 cup of Brazil nuts & 2 cloves of garlic well blended in a food processor works a treat on the Paleo diet)
- raw salt & black pepper to taste.

*If desired you can add 1/2 cup cooked gluten free pasta shells.

Directions:

1. Preheat oven to 375F (180C)
2. Grease a 9-inch casserole dish with coconut or olive oil.
3. Place all ingredients except the cheese into a large bowl. Mix until well combined.
4. Transfer into a suitable casserole dish and Sprinkle the cheese mix over the top (this can be done after cooking instead).
5. Bake for about 35-45 minutes or until casserole is holding in the middle.
6. Sprinkle with additional parsley or herbs if desired.

This tastes really nice cold as well as hot. Be sure the lunch box is chilled.

EASY MINI QUICHES

These obviously aren't for kids with allergies, but you may be able to adapt to suit your own needs. You may want to play with egg replacers.

The variety is vast when it comes to making mini quiches or tarts. Even though they are divine hot for lunches, many taste nice cold in a lunch box too. Buy pastry from the supermarket if you want, do what works for you because time is often a problem with children and work commitments! Just grab whatever pastry you prefer and your son or daughter likes. Pasties vary and so do the sizes of little pie tins, so experiment to start with. I find silicon muffin trays don't brown on the bottom like tin pans.

Here are some mini quiche combinations to try if your child likes egg - Be imaginative:

-egg - cheese - spinach - mushroom
-egg - feta - nutmeg
-egg - garlic - ham - fetta
-cooked beef mince - spring onion - egg
-egg - leftover vegetables - cheese
-grated carrot - egg - nutmeg - feta
-bacon - egg - tomato - cheese
-egg - pine nuts - baby spinach
-egg - cooked chicken - corn - parsley
-egg - tuna - cream cheese - corn
-egg - mashed pumpkin - nutmeg
-egg - cooked chicken - cheese - parsley
-egg - tomato - sardines - cheese - olives

-cheese - corn - peas - salami
-egg - garlic - grated zucchini - parmesan
-egg - bacon - spinach - basil
-egg - ham - olives - spinach

CRUSTLESS ZUCCHINI TARTLETS

This recipe isn't strictly Paleo but thought it was worth including. Try substituting for Paleo friendly milk, cream and flour ingredients if desired.

Ingredients for frying:

- 1 Tbsp olive oil
- 1 - 2 cloves garlic, minced
- 2 shallots or spring onions, diced
- 2 small zucchinis, grated (chopped spinach or kale works too)
- 1/4 cup grated Parmesan cheese

Ingredients for batter:

- 1 1/4 cup milk
- 1/4 cup cornstarch (cornflour)
- 2 large eggs
- 2 large egg yolks
- 1 cup cream
- 3/4 tsp raw salt
- chopped fresh herbs if desired

Directions: *Preheat oven to 350F (180C)* Grease or line 2 mini muffin or standard muffin tins.

Zucchini Mixture Directions:

1. *Heat a pan to medium. Add oil, garlic and shallots and stir for about 2 minutes.*
2. *Add the grated zucchini, and stir until just softened, another few minutes. Remove from heat.*

Batter Mixture Directions:

1. *Whisk 1/2 cup of the milk into the cornstarch, mixing until smooth.*
2. *Whisk in all the eggs mixing until smooth, then gradually whisk in the rest of the milk, the cream, salt, and any seasonings.*

Assembly:

1. *Put a pinch of cheese into each muffin cup, a teaspoon of the zucchini mix and herbs if desired.*
2. *Now pour 1 Tbsp of the batter mix over the top into each muffin cup, filling almost to the top.*
3. *Bake until the tarts start to turn a golden color, about 12 - 15 mins.*

Allow to cool. A wonderfully nutritious lunch idea hot or cold. These freeze well too.

HONEY CINNAMON CARAMELIZED NUTS

Ingredients:

- 1 cup raw cashew nuts
- 1 cup raw walnuts
- ¼ cup raw honey
- 1 tsp cinnamon

Directions:

1. *In a bowl mix together the nuts.*
2. *Add the honey and cinnamon to thoroughly coat the nuts.*

Preheat oven to 350°F (180°C) or can try cooking in the slow cooker on low heat for about 2 hours.

1. *Put some baking paper on a baking sheet and evenly spread the nuts across it.*
2. *Roast for about 15 - 25 minutes until they are golden brown. Stir every 10 minutes or so to brown evenly.*
3. *Great addition to any lunch box or as a party snack.*

EGGPLANT CHIPS

If you want to eat these not as crisp but with lunch at home, just don't cook them in the oven for as long. Cook on the stove top. Sweet potato and pumpkin is also good like this.

Ingredients:

- 1 large eggplant, sliced (pumpkin and potato works too)
- 2 Tbsp olive oil
- salt and ground black pepper to taste. Can get creative and add some sesame seeds or dried herbs.

Directions:

1. *Preheat the oven to 275°F (135°C).*
2. *Slice the eggplant, and put the slices on a baking sheet. Sprinkle the eggplant slices with salt and drizzle with oil.*
3. *Bake in the oven for about 30-40 minutes. Turn the slices around every 10-15 minutes until they are crisp.*
4. *The eggplant chips can be eaten just as they are or served as crackers with various dips or spreads.*

HONEY GLAZED DRUMSTICKS

Great for lunch or the lunch box!

Ingredients:

- 4 chicken drumsticks
- 2 Tbsp tomato ketchup
- 2 tsp olive oil
- 1 Tbsp honey or Maple syrup
- 1 tsp Worcestershire sauce
- 2 tsp lemon juice

Directions:

1. *Dry the excess moisture off the chicken with paper towel.*
2. *Make deep incisions over the drumsticks with a sharp knife.*

3. *Put all the ingredients in a large bowl and mix together.*
4. *Place the chicken in the bowl and leave in the refrigerator for at least an hour, but preferably overnight to marinate. Turn occasionally.*
5. *Heat the oven to 400 F (200 C) and place chicken on a baking sheet. Cover loosely with aluminum foil.*
6. *Cook for about 20 min, then remove the foil, baste the chicken again then return back to the other for a further 15 min or until the juices run clear and the chicken is cooked.*
7. *Once the drumsticks have cooled completely, wrap a small piece of foil around each leg so it is easy to handle.*

Wrap individually with a nonstick baking paper and then foil and place them in the refrigerator.

PALEO LEMON & POPPY SEED MUFFINS

Ingredients:

- 1/2 cup coconut flour
- 3/4 cup raw honey (or substitute with fruit puree, maple syrup or agave nectar)
- 1/4 cup coconut oil
- 4 large eggs
- 1 large lemon
- zest of 1 lemon
- 2 drops of Bergamot essential oil (optional...I like the flavor)
- 2 Tbsp poppy seeds (can use chia seeds instead)
- 1 Tbsp vanilla extract
- 1/2 tsp baking soda

Directions:

1. *Preheat the oven to 325°F (160°C) Grease or prepare a muffin tin with liners.*
2. *Juice and zest the lemon.*
3. *Combine the eggs, vanilla, bergamot oil, lemon zest and juice together in a large bowl. Set aside.*
4. *In a small saucepan heated to low, melt together the honey and oil.*
5. *Stir this into the egg mix.*
6. *In another bowl mix together the flour, poppy seeds and baking soda.*
7. ***SLOWLY fold in gently,*** *ONLY until the ingredients are just mixed.*
8. *Pour the batter in each cup until it is about half full.*
9. *Bake for 20-25 minutes or until a skewer comes out clean, less for mini muffins.*

LUNCHBOX BEEF JERKY

The boys love this one for a snack! Experiment with this recipe due to the different variables in meat thickness and oven temps. Start early in the day due to long cooking times. (A food dehydrator can be used instead of oven) Spices, herbs and pepper are tasty but optional.

Ingredients:

- 1lb (450g) beef sirloin steak, cut into thin slices a few inches long.
- ½ cup coconut aminos (or soy sauce)

Directions:

1. *Trim any fat from the meat, then put it in the freezer for 30 - 60 mins to firm up.*
2. *Remove the steak from the freezer and with a sharp knife cut the meat against the grain. Make the slices very thin, but keep them as evenly sized as possible so drying time is equal. The bigger they are, the longer drying time will be.*
3. *Put the beef pieces and oil in a large plastic bag.*
4. *Let the beef marinate overnight or at least for few hours.*
5. *Preheat the oven to 160 F (70 C) for dehydrating the jerky. Leave the oven door slightly ajar with a teaspoon.*
6. *Use absorbent paper toweling to mop up any excess oil from the meat.*
7. *There are several ways to cook the meat - Place into a food dehydrator (this is what I do) and cook for about 12 hours on the meat setting.*
   OR thread one end of each piece of meat onto skewers, placing sideways in oven and allow to hang with a pan catching any drips underneath, or line two baking sheets with aluminum foil, place racks on top of them so the jerky would be exposed to hot air on both sides.
8. *Place the jerky onto the racks. Keep them slightly separate to make them accessible to air and dry evenly.*
9. *Bake for about 8 - 12 hours until dry but slightly pliable. Cool and store in an airtight container.*

COLD MINI TOAST TREATS

Either buy mini toasts from the supermarket or make your own by cutting up squares of bread, drizzle with a little oil and pop in the oven until crisp. These are great when you need something flexible for the lunch box. Have a bag of toasts in the pantry at the ready, and a cooler. When cool, add a slice of cheese, dip, or cream cheese on the bottom and top with anything your child likes. Get creative! **Here are a few favorite ideas for the toppings:**

cheese - ham - watercress
avocado spread (with a little lemon juice) - tomato
cheese - bacon - grated cucumber
cream cheese - gherkin
hummus - grated carrot - basil
cream cheese - sweet chili sauce - parsley
cheese - cooked cold meat - dip

EASY RICE BUBBLE SLICE

Don't buy those unhealthy high sugar, high fat sweet rubbishy bars from the supermarket! This may be a sweet treat, but you know exactly what is in it.

Ingredients:

- 130g butter
- 1/4 cup sugar
- 3 Tbs natural honey
- 3 tsp sesame seeds
- 1/2 tsp vanilla extract
- 5 cups rice bubbles or similar low sugar rice cereal

* Stealth bomb coming up...2 tsp chia seeds and crushed walnuts or macadamia nuts.

Directions:

1. *Line a sandwich baking tray with baking paper.*
2. *Place the butter and sugar into a saucepan and bring to the boil. Stir in honey and boil for another 3 mins. Stir in vanilla and sesame seeds. Remove from the heat. Stir in rice bubbles then immediately pour into the lined tray.*
3. *Press down the mixture flat with a rubber spatula or spoon then allow to set.*

BACON WRAPPED CHICKEN

This recipe is easy, you just need to make the chicken pieces fairly uniform in size, otherwise allow the larger pieces to cook for longer.

Ingredients:

- Use boneless chicken cut into bite sized pieces.
- Use bacon sliced into pieces large enough to wrap around the chicken pieces

Quantity will depend on how much you want to cook and size. (Use about 2 chicken breasts to 3 rashers of bacon)

Directions:

1. *Preheat the oven to medium high 375 F (190 C)*
2. *Cut chicken into pieces.*
3. *Cut bacon into strips and firmly wrap around the chicken.*
4. *Secure each wrap with toothpicks (both ends)*
5. *Bake in a medium hot oven till golden brown, about half an hour.*

Pack up chilled with a salad and/or fruit. Yum!

EASY HOMEMADE HUMMUS

This is a non Paleo lunch idea. Another flexible recipe. Experiment with your child's favorite flavors!

Ingredients:

- 1 small can of bought cooked chickpeas, about 200 g or 14oz, drained and rinsed
- 4 Tbsp of your favorite soft cheese (even cheddar is okay - try coconut cream for dairy free)
- 1 Tbsp olive or macadamia oil
- 1 Tbsp lemon juice
- 1/2 clove minced garlic
- 1/2 tsp of your favorite ground spice such as cumin seed or nutmeg (optional)
- salt and pepper to taste

Directions:

1. *Blend all ingredients in the food processor until smooth, scraping down the sides as you go.*
2. *Divided into individual containers ready for the lunchbox or fridge and keep chilled.*

PRUNES WRAPPED IN BLANKETS

Ingredients:

- 12 pitted prunes (figs work too)
- 12 almonds, toasted or raw (optional)
- 6 thin slices bacon

* The almond surprise in the middle make a nice addition.

Directions:

1. *Heat oven to 450 F (230C)*
2. *Put an almond in each pitted prune, where the stone was.*
3. *Cut the bacon in half and wrap a piece of it around each prune.*

Secure with a cocktail toothpick.
4. Place on a baking sheet and cook until the bacon is crisp, about 10 minutes. You will need to turn it.
5. Lunch box delight for boys and girls, adults too!

EASY SPICY CRAB MEAT DIP

On occasion when we go fishing we are lucky enough to catch crayfish or lobster, and this is ideal in this delicious dip. You can also use canned tuna or salmon, but drain it well first.

Ingredients:

- 1 tsp lemon juice
- 1/2 tsp tomato paste
- 2 Tbsp homemade or natural mayonnaise
- 1 large gherkin or pickled onion, finely diced
- 3 drops of fish sauce (optional)
- 1 small can of white crab meat, about 5 ounces or 120 g. If you can get fresh...all the better!

Directions:

1. *Blend all ingredients well in a food processor except the crabmeat.*
2. *Stir in the crab- meat to the chunky consistency you want.*
3. *Divide into airtight containers, be sure to keep this dip well chilled and have crackers or toast with it.*

THE END

SUGGESTED GOOD READS

Kid's nutrition and health can benefit from making smoothies and juices at home. They are fabulous partly frozen as a chiller pack and cold drink in the lunch box.

Here are some suggested good reads regarding super juices and smoothies, how to detect hidden sugars in foods and read labels, and the immunity system.

- *Juicer Recipes to Treat Common Health Ailments & Boost Immune* by Jane Burton

- *Paleo Smoothies* by Jane Burton

- *Low Sugar Diet* book by Peggy Annear

- *School Time Recipes* by Alisa Marie Fleming

- *Super Immunity and Nutrition* by Joel Fuhrman

- Get a FREE copy of a *Paleo Desserts* book at http://paleorecipeblog.com

80CB

NOTES

COPYRIGHT

LUNCH BOX RECIPES ©2014 JANE BURTON

Made in the USA
Middletown, DE
15 April 2017